A HANDBO

RHETORIC

AND

PROSODY

JAYDIP SARKAR

ANINDYA BHATTACHARYA

Orient BlackSwan

A Handbook of Rhetoric and Prosody
_____

Orient Blackswan Private Limited

Registered Office
3-6-752 Himayatnagar, Hyderabad 500 029, Telangana, India
Email: centraloffice@orientblackswan.com

Other Offices
Bengaluru, Chennai, Guwahati, Hyderabad, Kolkata
Mumbai, New Delhi, Noida, Patna, Visakhapatnam

© Orient Blackswan Private Limited 2018
First published 2018
Reprinted 2020, 2022

Cover and book design
© Orient Blackswan Private Limited 2018

033936

ISBN 978-93-5287-277-0

Typeset in Minion Pro 11/13 *by*
Bookcraft Publishing Services (I) Private Limited, Chennai 600 028

Printed at
Yashprintographics, Noida. -201301

Published by
Orient Blackswan Private Limited
3-6-752 Himayatnagar, Hyderabad 500 029, Telangana, India
Email: info@orientblackswan.com

For

RAI *and* IRARUPA

Our dear daughters

Contents

Preface

Rhetoric and prosody are usually thought of as the arts of analysing aesthetic language use. However, they were strongly rooted in the political and civic life of the classical world, and they remain so, albeit differently, in the intellectual life of the major democracies of the world. Rhetoric and prosody constitute an intricate and interesting area of study that students of English language and literature ought to familiarise themselves with in their beginning years. Literary appreciation and criticism, as well as analyses of sociopolitical and media discourses, are not possible without a sound knowledge of these special kinds of language use. *A Handbook of Rhetoric and Prosody* offers students a guided tour of the evolution and use of rhetorical tropes and techniques. Its approach aligns the book closely with the history of English literature, and draws a smooth learning curve for beginners.

We take this opportunity to acknowledge the intellectual and personal debts we incurred to Dr Chandanashis Laha, Professor at the Department of English, University of North Bengal. He is our constant inspiration. We sincerely thank James Kanjamala, Senior Editor at Orient Blackswan. His long experience in the field played a critical role in the development of this book from the manuscript stage to its present form. In the eighth chapter of the 'Rhetoric' section, we have used some lines from his unpublished translation of *Beowulf*.

We gift this book to our daughters Rai and Ira, who are the rhetoric and prosody of our lives.

Jaydip Sarkar and Anindya Bhattacharya
15 August 2017

RHETORIC

Introduction

RHETORIC: A BRIEF HISTORY

The term 'rhetoric' was first used in ancient Greece and referred to the art of effective language use, capable of persuading and motivating an audience. Greece was also the birthplace of democracy: a system where eloquent citizens of a city-state could influence political decisions. The English word 'rhetoric' derives from the Greek word *rhetor* which means 'speaker' or 'orator'. A *rhetor* was a master of persuasion—an ability that a citizen required at the assemblies of the city-state. As Conley observes, in the European tradition, a consensus of opinion has always been reached through open discussions and free public debate, even though participatory democracy was not always present (*Rhetoric in the European Tradition*).

Down the ages, 'rhetoric' acquired a related meaning. From 'persuasive civic discourse', it came to mean the *technê* (the Greek word for 'art', 'skill', or 'technique') of oratory—the study of the rules of effective language use. A speaker who wished to create a sense of communion with the audience would need to master the *technê* of rhetoric. The *skill* of public speaking could be taught and learnt.

'Rhetoric'—in the combined sense of oratorical performance as well as oratorical technique—is thus 'the discourse of citizens and subjects' trying to organise the world they inhabit. Rhetoric may be conservative or subversive; it may reinforce or counter contemporary narratives. However, it will always be social and historical as it expresses the episteme of a particular time and society (Habinek, *Ancient Rhetoric and Oratory*).

This introduction to rhetoric tries to inform the student of this tradition of responsible civic persuasion. Learning rhetoric does not mean the mere memorising of a set of universal rules, but undertaking a journey through history: the study of *technê* is effective when the student is aware of its tradition and evolution, from the days of the classical Greek rhetoricians to postmodern theorists.

The classical tradition

The sophists were the first to teach rhetoric in Greece. 'Sophists' were learned professors who taught the art of speech making and persuasion, and established rhetoric as necessary education for participation in civic life. However, over time they came to be seen as conceited and arrogant flatterers of audiences. This opinion was expressed by Plato, the founder of Western political philosophy, who did not favour the art of rhetoric. (He did not approve of poetry either, and excluded poets from his ideal republic.) In Plato's *Gorgias*, a Socratic dialogue written around 380 BCE, 'rhetoric' finds its third (and derogatory) meaning: it comes to signify empty and flowery verbiage; the deft use of high-flown language to please or flatter, apparently with a political intention. It is dishonest, immoral and dangerous. Plato's influential arguments cost the sophists a great deal of public respect. As a result, the art of rhetoric, just like poetry, would need many 'apologies' in the years to come.

Isocrates, one of the later sophists, responded to Plato's attack by moving away from both the sophist tradition as well as Plato's abstractions, and upheld rhetoric as a noble instrument in a nation's civic life. According to Isocrates, students needed rhetorical education not to achieve personal gains but for public service: it would help them become eloquent *and* responsible citizens of the state. Lessons in rhetoric would lead students to noble ideas, which in turn would lead to better policy-making.

Aristotle's *On Rhetoric: A Theory of Civil Discourse*, written intermittently in the fourth century BCE, reclaimed the art of rhetoric by playing down the moral element. As the book which provided the 'first comprehensive theory of rhetorical discourse' (Dillard and Pfau, *The Persuasion Handbook*), it focused purely on the *technê* of persuasion. In the first chapter of *Rhetoric*, Aristotle begins by defining rhetoric as the counterpart of dialectic, and thus one of the three key elements of philosophy (the third one being logic). The orator was morally responsible for his way of using the power of rhetoric.

The Hellenistic tradition of rhetoric was appropriated in later antiquity (fifth century BCE to fifth century CE) by the Roman schools of rhetoric, which used handbooks such as the anonymous *Rhetorica ad Alexandrum* (c. 340 BCE) and the *Rhetorica ad Herennium* (c. 85 BCE), as well as Horace's *Ars Poetica* (first century BCE). Oral and written persuasion became an essential element of the trivium (the three arts of language: grammar, logic and rhetoric), a vital part of advanced education in the Roman Empire.

The ethical and civic orientation of the study of rhetoric, and the kind of technical cataloguing of rhetorical devices that we see in today's handbooks, began in Aristotle's time and continued in the (Latin) writings of Roman rhetoricians near the first century BCE. Two individuals who stand out in this period are Cicero, a Roman statesman and orator remembered for his mastery of Latin prose, and Quintilian, a Roman teacher and lawyer. Cicero's *De Inventione* (c. 86 BCE) and *De Oratore* (55 BCE) pondered over the direct application of rhetoric in civic discourse, and were used to teach *rhetors* the art of structuration and composition in discourse. This theme was to be developed later in Quintilian's twelve-volume work *Institutio Oratoria* (c. 95 CE).

Cicero regarded Isocrates as his model and represented the figure of the unselfish statesman-orator as the guardian of the 'common good'. Cicero's myth of the origin of society—the eloquent sage persuading savages to live together peacefully—anticipates Rousseau's social contract theory. This image of a savage society is reiterated in Quintilian. His *Institutio* advocates a programme for educating citizens in oratory and morality. *De Oratore* and *Institutio* were to become two of the most influential texts in the fields of not only rhetoric but also political philosophy, and would make a profound impact on future pedagogy. These works powerfully argue that, in a time of deteriorating ethical standards, teaching rhetoric to future citizens and senators can save the state from destruction.

The classical tradition thus imagined the *vir civilis*, an ideal, insightful citizen, in command of the *technê* of persuasive speaking and responsible for the common good (Skinner, *Reason and Rhetoric in the Philosophy of Hobbes*). The epithet 'Ciceronian style' of rhetoric later came to be applied to the oratory of upright and respectable speakers who attacked the enemies of the state.

Medieval to early modern times

The classical stress on carefully structured urbane writing (*ars dictaminis*) continued in the medieval period and later in the Renaissance, which is evident in Philip Sidney's *A Defence of Poetry*.

Saint Augustine's *De Doctrina Christiana* (397–426 CE) was the first text of 'Christian rhetoric'—a new theological tradition which would harness the power of Cicero to bolster religious exhortation and interpretation. This new tradition of hermeneutics focussed on the responsible and 'true' interpretation of the scripture. Interestingly, this leads to a dualist semiotic theory which proposes that writing (the signifier) is different from spiritual/Christian 'truth' (the signified). Other important names that combined the pagan art of rhetoric with Christian theology are Boethius, Bede and Thomas Aquinas. Rhetoric was not completely rejected, but interpretation and the search for truth became supreme. The scholar therefore had to meditate on a particular passage to find out the spiritual truth which remains hidden behind the façade of language. It is not very hard to see how Plato's distrust of figurative language followed from a similar dualist philosophy.

There was renewed interest in the study of rhetoric during the Italian Renaissance. Greek texts found favour in the city-state of Florence, which resembled democratic Athens. Thus far, classical texts had been in the control of the clergy, who were often not equipped to decipher these texts. In the first quarter of the fifteenth century, many classical texts, such as *Institutio Oratoria*, *De Oratore* and *Brutus*, reached Renaissance scholars who brought out erudite editions of these texts. When these secular scholars started writing rhetorical treatises of their own, they emulated the 'ancient masters'. As a result, Renaissance rhetoric (and poetics) became an elaborate and complex project that sought to assimilate various strands of past narratives on rhetoric.

More importantly, the scholars who later came to be called 'humanists' were politically active people: Desiderius Erasmus, who spoke against the excesses of the Church, and Martin Luther and John Calvin, who led the Reformation, all took recourse to rhetoric to convert their audience to their unique views. Luther's *Ninety-Five Theses* (1517), Calvin's *Institutes of the Christian Religion* (1536), and Erasmus' works, including *The Praise of Folly* (1511) and *Ecclesiastes* (1535), used rhetoric to establish their points. A hot debate erupted when Erasmus attacked the Latin style of his contemporaries in *The Ciceronian* (1528), arguing that Cicero wrote in a pagan world, and using that style to interpret Christian texts is wrong. Many commentators participated in the ensuing exchange.

Humanists like Erasmus held that the faculty of expression helped one reach the ideal of humanity. His *Copia: Foundations of the Abundant Style* (1512) was a bestseller.

The popular desire to speak well in order to climb the social ladder was addressed by an abundant crop of manuals such as Philip Melanchthon's *Rhetoric* (1521) and Henry Peacham's *The Garden of Eloquence* (1577). George Puttenham's *The Art of English Poetry* (1589) points towards a hardening of a prescriptive attitude: 'style' and 'decorum' were increasingly attributed a central space in expression. To speak well and emotionally *move* people was a primary agenda of these books.

The turn towards *elocutio* (speaking well) was a significant characteristic of Renaissance rhetoric. Baldassare Castiglione's *Il Cortegiano* (1528)—translated into English as *The Courtier* (1561)—popularised *elocutio* as the basis of courtly culture. It became a course-book for the prospering middle classes in Tudor England who sought, somewhat unsuccessfully, to acquire aristocratic cultural codes through an elegant use of tropes in conversation. The writings of Petrus Ramus, a sixteenth-century French logician and rhetorician, exerted a powerful influence on the way rhetoric was viewed by later generations. In his works, he divorced rhetoric from logic. Thanks to the influential Ramist school of thought, rhetoric began to be seen as a matter of style and delivery alone.

The seventeenth century

Seventeenth-century England saw a renewed attack on rhetoric caused by major religious and political upheavals as well as major advances in scientific and socio-political enquiry. The period witnessed the beheading of the English monarch Charles I in 1649, followed by the rule of the republican regime of the Puritans for eleven years. The restoration of the monarchy in 1660 ushered in an age of peace and stability. The inflammatory rhetoric of ambitious men, which had led the nation to civil war, lost favour in public life. The volatility of the political climate and the supremacy accorded to reason and science led to fresh attacks on rhetoric. The term *copia* disappeared from political and civic discourses and was rehabilitated in the field of literary expression. The *elocutio* of previous generations was regarded as stilted and artificial language, and came to be detested in a cultural matrix that nurtured an increasing scientism, utilitarianism, as well as puritanism. In the words of Ben Jonson in 'An Epistle to Master John Selden':

Less shall I for the art of dressing care,
Truth, and the Graces, best when naked are.

The seventeenth-century rationalist metaphysical systems of Descartes, Spinoza and Leibniz exerted substantial influence on the philosophy of the Enlightenment. The advancement of the natural sciences was regarded as proof of the progress of civilisation and human emancipation. Isaac Newton's epoch-making treatise on physical phenomena, *Principia Mathematica* (1687), became the paradigm for scientists and empirical science. The arrival of the Newtonian universe meant a shift from a world of superstition to one of rational order and lucidity. Newton's system strongly advanced the Enlightenment discourses of order and reason. The French *Encyclopaedia* of Diderot and D'Alembert was dedicated to three empiricists—Francis Bacon, John Locke, and Isaac Newton, which indicates the ascendency of empiricism in the period.

The great figures of the Enlightenment were masters of rhetoric, yet, in some degree, suspicious of the influence of rhetoric on the public in a volatile age. Both Bacon and Locke rejected elaborate ornamentation in speech. Hobbes's *Leviathan* (1651) was written in exile in France. Apprehensive about the outcome of social discord, Hobbes connects rhetoric to rabble-rousing and inflammation of dangerous emotions. Ironically, the image of the great sea-beast leviathan (which Hobbes conjures up to represent the state) is itself a metaphor for the monarchy, and the whole discourse on its organisation (that the leviathan's head is the ruler, and the citizens, its body) is a fine example of persuasive rhetoric.

What we see here is a culmination of the dualist view of language as expressing either 'true', absolute knowledge or a biased, partisan point of view made plausible through the use of rhetoric. Stanley Fish mentions a long list of binaries that exist in the Western culture: fact/opinion, unmediated/mediated, clear/coloured, realities/illusions and so on. These rely on the underlying assumption that a clear, rational, unmediated truth exists which is the opposite of biased opinions, prejudices, points of view, or established cultural beliefs (*Doing What Comes Naturally*). A seeker after objective truth would use the '*neutral* observation language' (Thomas Kuhn quoted in Fish) which marks scientific discourse. A less privileged kind of discourse is the 'fine language' (Aristotle quoted in Fish) of a rhetorician, moulded by the preconceptions of the speaker, insidious in nature and intended to strategically 'charm the hearer' (ibid.).

This epistemological opposition, noted earlier in Aristotle and Plato, is clearly expressed in a famous attack on rhetoric by the Tory historian Thomas Sprat. His treatise *History of the Royal Society* (1667) denounces the inflammatory rhetoric of the Commonwealth years, celebrating the coming of the scientific culture of the Restoration era. His privileging of rational, dispassionate scientific expression over dubious rhetoric continued the debate over representation that began in the classical world:

> ... eloquence ought to be banish'd out of all civil Societies, as a thing fatal to Peace and good Manners. ... [The ornaments of speaking] are in open defiance against Reason; professing not to hold much correspondence with that; but with its Slaves, the Passions: they give the mind a motion too changeable, and bewitching, to consist with right practice. (quoted in Fish)

The demand of the new age was not Erasmus's *copia* but an unadorned and plain style which would make sense.

A counter-argument was advanced by Milton in *Areopagitica* (1644), subtitled 'A speech ... for the liberty of unlicensed printing, to the parliament of England'. It showed that 'responsible' persuasion need not be pacifist all the time: inflammatory or revolutionary rhetoric is essential to fight oppression. Milton not only drew upon his elaborate classical learning to develop his *technê*—the 'grand style' for *Paradise Lost*—but also accepted the classical ethics of an active citizen's life in politics. This spirit is summed up in the final sentence of *Areopagitica*, 'Give me liberty to know, to utter, and to argue freely according to conscience, above all liberties.'

The general perspective of the seventeenth century followed Ramus's notion that argument and proof belonged to the domain of logic/dialectic, not rhetoric. Rhetoric dealt with style. Rhetoric was no longer concerned with the discovery of knowledge, but only with the *communication* of knowledge. This trend continued throughout the Enlightenment.

The eighteenth century

The eighteenth century was one of the 'most prolific eras in rhetorical history' (Golden and Corbett, *The Rhetoric of Blair, Campbell and*

Whately) as there were remarkable shifts in the theory of rhetoric which challenged the classical paradigm of rhetoric as persuasion. If this century heard celebrated public speakers such as Thomas Paine, Edmund Burke and Adam Smith, it also embraced the belletristic movement which brought about an aestheticisation of rhetoric at the expense of its political role: rhetoric increasingly came to be seen as the art of literary ornamentation instead of civic persuasion.

A vital eighteenth-century belief was that an orderly and rational modern universe was to replace the earlier world of religious and political strife. Out of this cultural climate grew a new position that the foundation for a peaceable national life must be a new rationality and moderation instead of emotional outpourings and religious zeal. To describe any piece of writing or speech as 'imaginative' or 'visionary' was to severely criticise it as irresponsible and dangerous for the body politic.

In his *Epistle to Dr Arbuthnot*, Alexander Pope looked back on the modest times of his father, which was 'Stranger to civil and religious rage'. Civic persuasion was now seen as plain demagoguery. This was possibly the first time in history that unheroic social life was celebrated as exemplary. Detachment from politics, the absence of religious zeal, keeping a low profile, and shunning heroic braveries were deemed positive virtues in the post-Civil War era. Samuel Johnson warned against the 'dangerous prevalency of the imagination'. Instead, these men preferred the unheroic social virtues of 'good sense' and a lack of ambition. After the prolonged era of bloodshed and unrest, a period of lull was quite expected. Pope saw 'Reason' (a mental faculty that restrains ambition and self-seeking behaviour) as the governing moral faculty of a balanced individual. This apotheosis of low public visibility was inimical to the idea of the ideal citizen of the classical republic trained in the art of persuasion. The placidity of the citizen is encoded in a word that is ubiquitous in the literature of the period: 'Nature'. Pope invokes it in *An Essay on Criticism*:

> First follow Nature, and your judgement frame
> By her just standard, which is still the same.
> Unerring Nature, still divinely bright,
> One clear, unchanged, and universal light,
> Life, force, and beauty, must to all impart,
> At once the source, and end, and test of art.

The eighteenth century devised a closely guarded path for rhetoric: poetic expression has to 'follow nature', that is, depict the inherent, universal reasonableness and 'good sense' of man and impart prescribed norms to all. This poem announces the coming of literary criticism which would employ a 'proper', disciplined rhetoric, shorn of 'false eloquence'. Pope's prescription aptly sums up the highly moral role expected of an author in the eighteenth century: he was to preach sensibility and reasonableness in unadorned language and without flights of fancy.

'Gentility' was a powerful discourse in the eighteenth-century urban society of fashionable beaux and belles. As an attribute of the upper class, and a means of social differentiation, gentility demanded from the citizen a minimum standard of refinement and elegance in manner and expression. 'Self-improvement' through private study and writing, and developing a refined taste and style, became important. Over time the focus shifted from preparing to speak well in public fora to refining oneself for social advancement. Increased social mobility and the emergence of coffee-houses and numerous clubs helped push this trend forward. A consequent aestheticisation of rhetoric followed these developments.

This 'aestheticisation of rhetoric' is seen best in the late eighteenth-century belletristic movement headed by Hugh Blair, Richard Whately, and others. It offered an alternative to the classical tradition of rhetoric by expanding the scope of rhetoric to include the 'polite arts' such as poetry, drama, and even biography and history. Blair's *Lectures on Rhetoric and Belles Lettres* (1783) established rhetoric as a literary art. In this collection, the majority of lectures deal with 'taste', 'language' and 'style', while few elaborate on the civic function of rhetoric, with plenty of advice against false eloquence. The belletristic school, with its focus on the appreciation of good writing, leaned in to the general historical movement away from speech towards writing. Rhetoric was less about studying the skills of persuasion, and more about studying the effects of good writing for personal refinement and leisure.

Rhetoric, seen as the art of using tropes, that is, non-literal, figurative, embellished language, was often deemed to be against scientific clarity—the quest for 'truth' as it is—the basic premise of modernity. Giambattista Vico's 1708 lecture at the University of Naples, *On the Study Methods of Our Time*, was a landmark text that famously denounced the predominance of scientism in the university classroom that was a legacy of Bacon and Descartes. While not opposing the advance of scientific enquiry, it spoke out against its eroding effects on the *sensus communis*—the cultural-ethical conglomeration of ideas that form the political base of a community.

The nineteenth century

There was a general decline in the position of classical rhetoric in the nineteenth century as Romanticism reacted against strict eighteenth-century rules in composition and preferred spontaneous expression. The prefaces, apologies and letters written by nineteenth-century authors created the myth of Romantic originality and simple language. However, one must keep in mind the classical schooling of these writers, and their predilection for classical literature. Later commentators such as Bloom (*Anxiety of Influence*) and McFarland (*Originality and Imagination*) were critical of the notion of originality, and, after 'The Death of the Author', the idea became a burden.

The Romantic poets were not turning away from rhetoric: they were only putting it to use in a different way. While moving away from the technical acrobatics of neo-classicism, the Romantic poets moulded traditional rhetorical and poetic practices to suit their own poetic interests (Bialostosky and Needham): from neoclassical craft, dry wit and clarity of expression to the creation of an inspired and magical utterance. An interesting case is Wordsworth's use of personification and apostrophe to confer speech on nature, to have them testify, and to make them respond to his invocation (Kneale, *Romantic Aversions: Aftermaths of Classicism in Wordsworth and Coleridge*). Rhetoric here is inseparably intertwined with his profound philosophy of nature.

Later developments

The study of rhetoric, from the time of Plato and Aristotle, was based on a dualist view of language: the *literal* language of the philosopher and the scientist that could faithfully communicate the truth, versus the *figurative* language of the sophist and the rhetorician which was coloured by personal agenda. Friedrich Nietzsche's 'Description of Ancient Rhetoric'—the notes he compiled for his 1872–73 lecture series on ancient rhetoric at the

University of Basel—challenged the power relationship underlying this binary formation of literal–figurative in which the former was prioritised by Western culture.

The word 'composition' suggests, as Hillis Miller argues, a consciousness in control of the creation of meaning ('Nietzsche in Basel: Writing Reading'). This consciousness focuses all argument towards the one 'truth' of the discourse. This 'truth' is supposedly unadulterated by ideological or historical conditioning. However, Nietzsche's lectures invalidated the concept of perfectly translatable literal or 'proper' language that was superior to tropes or figurative meanings.

Nietzsche erased the traditional boundary between literal and figurative language, reiterating in his later writing that all language was necessarily figurative. The teleological quest was pointless: it assumed, under the influence of philosophers such as Locke and others, that the human mind can directly represent the pure truth about any object of rational enquiry. However, such representations were always mediated and edited by the mental acts of perception, conception, and linguistic representation. In his essay 'On Truth and Lie in an Extra-Moral Sense', Nietzsche defines truth as constantly changing representations—a horde of nomadic tropes. Using a famous image, he compares truth to a worn-out coin, the symbolic value of which has been forgotten.

'Rhetoric' became an interdisciplinary term with the publication of Kenneth Burke's *A Rhetoric of Motives* (1950) and *The Rhetoric of Religion* (1961), James L. Guetti's *The Rhetoric of Joseph Conrad* (1960), and Wayne Booth's *The Rhetoric of Fiction* (1961). In contemporary rhetorical theory, Kenneth Burke stands out as the most influential rhetorical theorist of the twentieth century. Burke's *A Rhetoric of Motives* (1950) and other subsequent works ascribe, like Vico, the demise of rhetorical study to the rise of scientism and the epistemological project driven by a desire for what is true in itself (Comas, 'Rhetoric'). However, unlike Vico or Nietzsche, Burke was not attempting an anti-modern rhetoric. He believed that it was the study of rhetoric, and not science, which could understand the *sensus communis*. Human beings are 'symbol-using animals'. All human activities are symbols, just like speech or writing. Every social activity is 'rhetorical' in this sense. Burke's 'new rhetoric' moved away from the classical tradition as he focused not on persuasion but on the social and symbolic uses of language, from political speeches and protest movements to music, art and architecture, and the rhetoric of religion and science.

The study of rhetoric began to align itself with linguistics. With Heidegger, Foucault and Lyotard, the theory of rhetoric as persuasion was abandoned. Postmodern rhetorical practices destabilised concepts such as presence, identity and the unity of meaning, rendering unambiguous human communication impossible. In principle, postmodern discourse regards all levels of language, referentiality and meaning as figurative: more 'tropical' than 'logical'. Language is now considered an attribute of the symbolic order of society, and the speaker's creation of meaning is contingent on the changing discursive nexus in which he finds himself.

FIGURES OF SPEECH

A figure of speech is a literary device which employs uncommon and unexpected language in order to send a semantically rich message which plain and simple language would fail to encode. After the above discussion, it is pointless to recreate the old binary of literal–figurative language—all language use is figurative. However, we shall differentiate between plainer language which fails to surprise the reader, and figurative language which has a greater impact on readers.

Figures of speech are traditionally divided into two classes: **tropes** and **schemes**.

The word 'trope' is derived from the Greek word for 'turn'. Tropes 'turn' or alter the meaning of words. A synecdoche, in which a part of something is used to signify a whole—for example, 'all *hands*' to mean 'all *men*'—is an example of a trope. The literal meaning of 'hands' has been altered to now signify 'men' in this context. Other examples of tropes include metaphor, metonymy, irony, simile and personification.

Schemes (derived from the Greek word for 'form') embellish language by affecting only the form of a sentence or phrase (for example, the arrangement of its words) without altering its meaning. A chiasmus—parallel clauses with their corresponding words reversed (for example, 'Fair is foul, and foul is fair')—is an example of a scheme.

For the sake of convenience, we may categorise figures of speech into the following groups.

GROUP 1   *Figures based on analogy, agreement or similarity*: simile, metaphor

GROUP 2   *Figures based on association*: metonymy, synecdoche, transferred epithet (hypallage), allusion

GROUP 3   *Figures based on difference or contrast*: antithesis, epigram, oxymoron, climax, anticlimax, bathos, syllepsis (condensed sentence), paradox

GROUP 4   *Figures based on imagination*: personification, prosopopoeia, personal metaphor, pathetic fallacy, apostrophe, invocation, vision, hyperbole

GROUP 5   *Figures based on indirectness*: innuendo, irony, sarcasm, periphrasis (circumlocution), euphemism, meiosis, litotes

GROUP 6   *Figures based on emotion*: erotesis (interrogation), exclamation

GROUP 7   *Figures based on construction*: hendiadys, chiasmus, ellipsis, zeugma, polysyndeton, asyndeton, hyperbaton (inversion), anaphora (epanaphora), epistrophe (epiphora)

GROUP 8   *Figures based on sound*: alliteration, consonance, assonance, pun (paronomasia), onomatopoeia

GROUP 9   *Miscellaneous figures*: tautology, pleonasm, prolepsis, paraleipsis, catachresis, ornamental epithet, aposiopesis

ONE

Figures based on Analogy, Agreement or Similarity

SIMILE

The term 'simile' is derived from the Latin word for 'similar'. A simile clearly states the similarity existing between two different entities.

The definition contains three elements.

- First, the things compared must be *different in kind.*
- Next, there must be *similarity* existing between the two different things. This is *the point of comparison.*
- Finally, the similarity must be *expressed clearly* through the use of words such as *like, as, so, such, similarly,* etc.

Common similes include phrases such as 'black as soot', 'ugly as a toad', 'soft as down', 'light as a feather', 'white as snow', 'hard as stone', 'ferocious as a tiger'. 'A simile, to be perfect', wrote Dr Johnson, 'must both illustrate and ennoble the subject; must show it to the understanding in a clearer view, and display it to the fancy with greater dignity: but either of these qualities may be sufficient to recommend it.'

Consider, for example, the following lines from Coleridge's ballad 'The Rime of the Ancient Mariner':

> The bride hath paced into the hall,
> Red as a rose is she ...

- Two different entities are compared to each other: a woman ('bride') and a rose
- The point of comparison: The bride is beautiful (= 'red'); the rose is a beautiful flower
- The comparison is clearly stated: the bride is 'red *as* a rose'

In the same poem, another simile is introduced by the expression 'as … as':

> Day after day, day after day,
> We stuck, nor breath nor motion;
> As idle as a painted ship
> Upon a painted ocean.

- Two different entities are compared to each other: a real ship and a ship drawn in a painting
- The point of comparison: a painted ship is motionless (= 'idle'); the speaker's ship stands still
- The comparison is clearly stated: one ship is '*as* idle *as*' the other

Next, let us consider the following lines from William Wordsworth's 'London, 1802':

> Thy soul was like a Star, and dwelt apart:
> Thou hadst a voice whose sound was like the sea:
> Pure as the naked heavens, majestic, free,
> So didst thou travel on life's common way …

In this sonnet on the city of London, Wordsworth criticises the contemporary socio-political life of England. Wordsworth feels that the age needed a staunch defender of liberty such as John Milton, the ideal poet and citizen. In the first three lines of the extract, Wordsworth uses three similes (highlighted above) to convey Milton's greatness. Look at the first one:

> Thy soul was like a Star, and dwelt apart

- Two different entities are compared to each other: Milton's genius (= 'thy soul') and a star
- The point of comparison: distance; just as a star is far above the earth, he was far above the petty political squabbles of his time
- The comparison is clearly stated: Milton's soul/genius 'was *like* a' distant star, superior to the rest of humanity

In the next simile—'Thou hadst a voice whose sound was like the sea'—the point of comparison is profoundness: Milton's poetry (= 'voice'), with its classical richness and depth, can be compared to the deep sound of sea waves. In the final simile—'Pure as the naked heavens, majestic, free / So didst thou travel on life's common way'—there are multiple points of comparison: Milton's mind was as open and wide (that is, liberal) as the majestic sky, and he was a champion of personal freedom. Try and analyse these two similes step by step, following the example above.

Let us look at a few more examples of similes.

> I wandered lonely as a cloud. (Wordsworth, 'I Wandered Lonely as a Cloud')

- The poet compares himself to a drifting cloud.
- The point of comparison: solitude
- The comparison is introduced by 'as'.

> And oft alone in nooks remote
> We meet thee, like a pleasant thought,
> When such are wanted. (Wordsworth, 'To the Daisy')

- The addressee (a daisy) is compared to a pleasant thought.
- The point of comparison: both of them bring a pleasant feeling to the poet in solitude
- The comparison is introduced by 'like'.

> Fear at my heart, as at a cup,
> My life-blood seemed to sip! (Coleridge, 'The Rime of the Ancient Mariner')

- The speaker's heart is compared to a cup.
- The point of comparison: both the heart and the cup are containers
- The comparison is introduced by 'as'.

> And ice mast-high came floating by
> As green as emerald. (Coleridge, 'The Rime of the Ancient Mariner')

- Ice is compared to emeralds.
- The point of comparison: colour ('green')
- The comparison is introduced by 'as ... as'.

> Like a child from the womb, like a ghost from the tomb,
> I arise and unbuild it again. (Shelley, 'The Cloud')

- The poetic persona (the cloud) compares itself to (1) a child, and (2) a ghost.
- The points of comparison: (1) birth, and (2) rebirth
- The comparisons are introduced by 'like'.

Sunbeam-proof, I hang like a roof ... (Shelley, 'The Cloud')

- The poetic persona (the cloud) compares itself to a roof.
- The point of comparison: both can shut out sunbeams
- The comparison is introduced by 'like'.

> The wedding guest stood still
> And listens like a three years' child. (Coleridge, 'The Rime
> of the Ancient Mariner')

- A listener (the 'wedding guest') is compared to a three-year-old child.
- The point of comparison: the rapt attention with which they listen to a story
- The comparison is introduced by 'like'.

> The holy time is quiet as a Nun
> Breathless with adoration ... (Wordsworth, 'It is a Beauteous
> Evening, Calm and Free')

- A moment in time is compared to a worshipping nun.
- The point of comparison: silence
- The comparison is introduced by 'as'.

> her name was like a summons to all my foolish blood
> (Joyce, 'Araby')

- The beloved's name is compared to a summons (a legal order to appear in person at a court).
- The point of comparison: compulsion that cannot be refused (just as one cannot ignore a summons from a court, the beloved's name evoked passions in the narrator which he couldn't deny or control)
- The comparison is introduced by 'like'.

> She walks in beauty, like the night
> Of cloudless climes and starry skies;
> And all that's best of dark and bright
> Meet in her aspect and her eyes

- A woman is compared to a cloudless, starry night.
- The point of comparison: striking beauty created by a juxtaposition of darkness and brilliance
- The comparison is introduced by 'like'.

The opening lines of Eliot's 'The Love Song of J. Alfred Prufrock' contain a memorable simile. The evening that descends upon a modern city is compared to an anaesthetised patient lying in an operation theatre; the point of comparison being the benumbed, lifeless nature of both the evening and the anaesthetised patient. It is a fitting image, in keeping with the premise and theme of the poem.

The following is an extract from Longfellow's 'Holidays':

> The sudden joys that out of darkness start
> As flames from ashes; swift desires that dart
> Like swallows singing down each wind that blows!
> White as the gleam of a receding sail,
> White as a cloud that floats and fades in air,
> White as the whitest lily on a stream,
> These tender memories are …

How many examples of simile can you trace in the above extract? Prepare a list of the objects/entities compared in each of these, and say what the points of comparison are. Ask your teacher for help.

Epic simile, or the Homeric simile

An epic simile is more than just a clear statement of similarity between two different things. A detailed and very elaborate comparison, an epic simile may run into several lines. Found typically in epic poetry, it is used to embellish and heighten the intensity of the emotion or the event being described. It is also referred to as a 'sustained simile' or an 'extended simile' because two or more comparisons follow one another, each usually building on the other and thus enriching an idea. The epic simile is also called the Homeric simile, as this device began in imitation of the protracted similes found abundantly in the *Iliad* and the *Odyssey*.

David Mikics, in *A New Handbook of Literary Terms*, observes that the epic simile conjures up a scene unconnected to the story of the poem, but familiar to the listeners/readers. The object of the simile is compared to an image that is usually foreign to the main plot of the epic. This image is developed independently of the narrative, and usually comes in the form 'Like a _____, when it _____.'

See, for example, Milton's use of the epic simile in Book I of *Paradise Lost* when Satan sees his army of angels, overwhelmed, floating on the fiery lake of the Hell:

His legions—Angel Forms, who lay entranced	(1)
Thick *as* autumnal leaves that strow the brooks	(2)
In Vallombrosa, where th' Etrurian shades	(3)
High over-arched embower; or scattered sedge	(4)
Afloat, when with fierce winds Orion armed	(5)
Hath vexed the Red-Sea coast, whose waves o'erthrew	(6)
Busiris and his Memphian chivalry,	(7)
While with perfidious hatred they pursued	(8)
The sojourners of Goshen, who beheld	(9)
From the safe shore their floating carcases	(10)
And broken chariot-wheels. *So* thick bestrown,	(11)
Abject and lost, lay these, covering the flood,	(12)
Under amazement of their hideous change.	(13)

- Object of the simile: the defeated fallen angels, lying stunned, floating on the lake of the Hell (Lines 1, 12)
- Simile introduced with: 'as' (Line 2)
- Comparison I: the fallen autumn leaves covering the streams of Vallombrosa valley (Lines 2–4)
- Comparison II: the drowned corpses of the Egyptian army floating on the Red Sea (Lines 4–11)
- Simile concluded with: 'so' (Line 11)
- Points of comparison: (a) large numbers, (b) fallen/defeated, (c) scattered and floating

In the above epic simile, the points to be noted are:

- The poet is wandering away from the main narrative, that is, the fall of the rebel angels.
- Vallombrosa valley in Italy and the biblical setting of the Exodus near the Red Sea are completely foreign to the cosmic background of *Paradise Lost*.
- The object of the simile (heaps of fallen angels) is unfamiliar to the listener/reader, while the things it is compared to (heaps of fallen leaves and the story of the defeat of the Egyptians) are more familiar.
- The two stories of Vallombrosa and the Exodus are digressions that are complete in themselves.

- These digressions do not advance the main plot. However, they are like an intricate design without which the story of the angels would become a bare outline.

In *Milton's English Poetry*, William Hunter is of the opinion that Milton's Vallombrosa simile surpasses the epic similes of Homer, Virgil, and Dante. The beauty of the evocatively described valley ironically counterpoints with the burning lake of Hell. Further, the image of a horde of fallen angels rolling in the lake is strengthened by another complex simile of the Pharaoh's army drowning in the Red Sea, which builds on the sense of destruction and confusion, and powerfully reinforces the idea of God's wrath.

Other epic similes from Book I of *Paradise Lost* include:

- The fallen angels, drawn up in battle order, are compared to the Egyptian plague of locusts.
- The huge bulk of Satan is compared to a great whale sleeping in the Arctic Sea.
- Satan is compared to Briareos, Typhon and Leviathan.
- Satan is compared to (a) the rising sun in a mist, and (b) the sun in an eclipse.

Similes such as these add to the grandeur of the epic style.

Guided exercise

Explain the nature of the comparison in the similes given below. The compared entities are indicated. Try to figure out the points of comparison.

1. The *Albatross* fell off, and sank
   Like *lead* into the sea.
   (Coleridge, 'The Rime of the Ancient Mariner')

2. Firm as a *rock* thy *truth* must stand.
   (Watts, 'Before Jehovah's Awful Throne')

3. Her *locks* were yellow as *gold*
   (Coleridge, 'The Rime of the Ancient Mariner')

4. The *childhood shows the man*,
   As *morning shows the day*. (Milton, *Paradise Regained*)

5. Higher still and higher
   From the earth *thou* springest
   Like a *cloud* of fire (Shelley, 'To a Skylark')

6. O my *love's* like a red, red *rose*
   That's newly sprung in June:
   O my *love's* like the *melody*
   That's sweetly played in tune. (Burns, 'A Red, Red Rose')

7. As *flies to wanton boys*, are *we to th' gods*,
   They kill us for their sport. (Shakespeare, *King Lear*)

8. And this grey spirit yearning in desire
   To follow *knowledge* like a *sinking star*,
   Beyond the utmost bound of human thought.
   (Tennyson, 'Ulysses')

9. And sometimes like a *gleaner thou* dost keep
   Steady thy laden head across the brook. (Keats, 'To Autumn')

10. All our household are at rest,
    The *hall* as silent as the *cell* (Coleridge, 'Christabel')

11. *She* dwelt among the untrodden ways ...
    Fair as a *star*, when only one
    Is shining in the sky.
    (Wordsworth, 'She Dwelt among the Untrodden Ways')

12. ... impressions poured in upon her ... and to follow *her thought*
    was like following *a voice which speaks too quickly* to be taken
    down by one's pencil ... (Woolf, *To the Lighthouse*)

13. Foolish curs, that run winking into the mouth of a Russian
    bear and have their *heads* crushed like *rotten apples*!
    (Shakespeare, *Henry V*)

14. Her *hair* that lay along her back
    Was yellow like *ripe corn*. (Rossetti, 'The Blessed Damozel')

15. *Glory* is like *a circle in the water*,
    Which never ceaseth to enlarge itself,
    Till, by broad spreading, it disperse to nought.
    (Shakespeare, *Henry VI*, Part I)

16. Like the *dew on the mountain*,
    Like the *foam on the river*,
    Like the *bubble on the fountain*,
    Thou art gone, and for ever! (Scott, 'Coronach')

17. And *life* ran gaily as the sparkling *Thames*
    (Arnold, 'The Scholar Gypsy')

18. These *words*, like *daggers*, enter in mine ears
    (Shakespeare, *Hamlet*)

19. Miserable, lonesome as a *forgotten child*, *she* sat in the quiet apartment ... (Fitzgerald, *The Beautiful and the Damned*)

20. *Misery* is manifold ... as the *rainbow*, its hues are as various as the hues of that arch. (Poe, 'Berenice')

METAPHOR

A 'metaphor' (derived from the Greek *metaphora*, meaning 'transfer') is a rhetorical device that transfers meaning from one field of reference to another.

The simplest form of metaphor is: 'A [first thing] *is* a [second thing]'. This can often lead to a situation that defies logic, and is not literally true. However, poetic truth differs from scientific truth. See, for example, the line:

Colonel Dutt is the lion of his battalion.

The above statement has a metaphorical sense which negates the literal meaning. Let us see what the statement does.

• It compares Colonel Dutt to a lion.
• The statement performs this feat by transferring meaning from an army unit to a different field: that of animal life in a forest. The lion is the king of the jungle, and Colonel Dutt is the leader of his military unit.
• It comments on the stature of the person: his leadership qualities, courage, strength, ferocity in battle, etc. The mention of a 'lion' brings to mind these qualities.
• The grounds for the comparison between Colonel Dutt and a lion is implied, instead of being introduced by words such as 'like', 'as', etc.
• The expression can be unpacked as a simile: 'Colonel Dutt is *as brave as* a lion' (or '*as strong as* a lion', or '*as fierce as* a lion', and so on).

Let us take up another simple metaphor.

America is a melting pot.

It is hard to imagine a country as a pot. However, the statement makes metaphorical sense. In the field of metallurgy, a melting pot is a vessel that is used to mix different metals. Here, the expression means that America offers an environment in which many ideas and races are socially assimilated. Let us see how the metaphor works.

- It compares America to a metallurgical crucible.
- It represents the social and cultural environment of America in a favourable light. Many ideas and races are assimilated there.
- The statement conveys this idea by transferring meaning from a socio-cultural reality to a different field: that of metallurgy. The result is that America is represented as a country with progressive and liberal values.
- The grounds for the comparison between America and a pot is implied, instead of being introduced by words such as 'like', 'as', etc.
- The expression can be unpacked as a simile: 'America is *like* a melting pot'.

A metaphor is far more powerful than a simile in that it can open the doors of the reader's imagination and create new worlds. For example, the line 'For Oliver, the school was a prison' would lose its evocative power if we turn it to a simile: 'For Oliver, the school was *like* a prison'. It would describe some outward reality and miss the mental distress of the little child.

When analysing metaphors, it is helpful to distinguish between two component elements: tenor and vehicle. The **tenor** is the subject of the metaphor, while the **vehicle** is the image or object to which the subject is compared. The tenor is what is being represented, what is being spoken of. The vehicle is that which represents the tenor; it is the object or idea whose attributes are applied to the tenor. In the first example above, Colonel Dutt is the tenor (the subject of the metaphor), while the vehicle is a lion (the object that the subject/tenor is compared to). Similarly, in the next two examples, 'America' and 'school' are the tenors, while 'melting pot' and 'prison' are their respective vehicles.

Constructing a metaphor

A metaphor can be expressed in many ways. A *noun* metaphor is the easiest to decipher. The tenor (subject of the comparison) and the vehicle (object it is compared to) are both mentioned, and the comparison usually follows the simple 'X is Y' formula.

He is the only hope of his family.

A person (the tenor) is compared to a family's expectations of the future (the vehicle). Goethe's *Elective Affinities* has another example of a metaphor constructed in this simple manner.

Behaviour is a mirror in which everyone displays his own image.

A tenor (behaviour) is directly compared to a vehicle (mirror), both being nouns. Nouns may also be directly compared using 'of', as in this line from Shakespeare's *Macbeth*:

The wine of life is drawn.

Here, life (the tenor) is compared to wine (vehicle), and the two nouns are connected using a simple 'X of Y' formula. Another way of comparing two nouns is by placing them side by side and connecting them using a simple possessive, as in this line from *Macbeth*:

After life's fitful fever he sleeps well.

Life (the tenor) is compared to a fever (vehicle)—both are characterised by suffering.

One has to exercise caution when a metaphor is expressed through a *verb*.

He failed to *bridle* his passions.

The verb 'bridle' means to control a horse by holding its reins. Here, a man's passions are compared to an unrestrained horse. Losing control over a horse is dangerous for the rider. In the same way, one has to keep one's emotions under control. The important thing to note here is that only the subject of the comparison (that is, the tenor: 'passions') is mentioned. The vehicle (an unbridled horse) is absent in the statement, and is understood through the use of a verb ('bridle') associated with the object. Here is another example of such a metaphor, from the story 'A Real Life' by Alice Munro:

She *drank in* admiration ...

The metaphor compares admiration (the tenor) with wine (the vehicle). However, the vehicle is not present in the line, and is understood through the implication of the verb 'drank in'. Such metaphors can be very expressive: the line points at the lady's sense of intoxication through idolisation.

A metaphor may also mention one of the two things being compared along with the *point of comparison*.

> She rescued him from the depths of despair.

Here, despair (the subject of the comparison) is compared to the sea (the object of the comparison). This object/vehicle is not mentioned, but is understood through the point of comparison ('depth') which is mentioned. Such metaphors identify a characteristic feature or quality of the object/vehicle and find it in the subject. In Shakespeare's *Hamlet*, the protagonist makes use of such a metaphor when he says:

> For who would bear the whips and scorns of time?

Time (the tenor) is compared to a tyrant (the vehicle). The vehicle is not explicitly mentioned, but may be identified through the phrase 'whips and scorns', the instruments of a tyrant. Time, therefore, is as cruel as a tyrant.

Finally, a metaphor can be expressed through an *adjective*.

> He missed a *golden* opportunity.

Here the comparison is between gold and an opportunity. The point of comparison is that both gold and an opportunity are valuable.

Let us examine a few more examples of metaphor.

> The curfew tolls the knell of parting day. (Gray, 'Elegy Written in a Country Churchyard')

- The statement compares a departed day (tenor) to a dead person (vehicle). The day, like the life of a person, has ended.
- The vehicle is not mentioned, but understood through the point of comparison.
- The point of comparison: Just as a man's death is announced by a knell, the end of the day is announced by the sound of the curfew.

- Transfer of meaning takes place from the field of everyday phenomena to that of funeral rituals.

    I will drink life to the lees. (Tennyson, 'Ulysses')

- Life (tenor) is compared to wine (vehicle).
- The object of the comparison (wine) is not mentioned but is understood through the use of the verb ('drink') as well as the use of the word 'lees' (the sediment of wine deposited at the bottom of a cup).
- The point of comparison: sweetness (Both wine and life are sweet.)
- Drinking 'life to the lees' implies enjoying one's life to the fullest.

    The committee shot her ideas down one by one.

- Ideas (tenor) are compared to fighter planes (vehicle) flying within the range of anti-aircraft guns.
- The object of the comparison (fighter aircraft) is not mentioned but is understood through the use of the phrasal verb 'shot down'.
- The point of comparison: Like low-flying aircraft, her ideas could not be defended.

    The detective dug up enough evidence to convict the suspect.

- The detective is likened to a dog.
- The object of the comparison (dog) is not mentioned but is understood through the use of the phrasal verb 'dug up'.
- The point of comparison: The detective unearthed hidden evidence like a dog smells and digs out buried bones.

    Our birth is but a sleep and a forgetting. (Wordsworth, 'Ode: Intimations of Immortality')

- The entirety of man's life on earth (tenor) is likened to a period of forgetful sleep (vehicle).
- Wordsworth believed that our souls exist in heaven prior to birth. An adult forgets his heavenly origin. Therefore, a man's life is like a sleep during which he does not remember where he came from. Death will wake him from this sleep.
- Here, two noun phrases are compared: man's life ('our birth') is likened to a period of sleep-like amnesia ('a sleep and a forgetting') using an 'X is Y' formula.

- Apart from metaphor, this line also contains two other rhetorical devices: **synecdoche** (see page 37) and **hendiadys** (see page 109). You will learn about these later.

Dead metaphor

Dead metaphors are expressions that have become so common through overuse that readers/listeners no longer think about the comparison being made. These metaphors are regarded as clichés. Some examples are: a ray of hope; a shade of doubt; the fire of passion; the light of knowledge; the reins of office; iron courage; a fiery speech; a lame excuse; a flash of wit; the gloom of despair; a flight of fancy.

Mixed metaphor

When two or more metaphors of different kinds are used together in dealing with the same subject, we get an instance of a mixed metaphor. The following line is from Shakespeare's *Hamlet*:

... to take arms against a sea of troubles

Confronting one's troubles is compared to going to war through the metaphor 'take arms against'. Another metaphor, 'a sea of troubles', conveys the enormousness of man's problems. However, using them together leads to an absurd image: one cannot wage war against a sea. Skilful writers like Shakespeare have, however, made effective use of mixed metaphors; but in the hands of lesser authors the incongruity of the metaphoric ideas leads to ludicrous imagery.

Extended metaphor, or sustained metaphor

In an extended metaphor, a single metaphor is sustained through a number of lines which explore the implications of the comparison or develop the central idea, in order to present a well-realised image. See, for example, the following lines from Shakespeare's *As You Like It*:

All the world's a stage,
And all the men and women merely players;
They have their exits and their entrances,
And one man in his time plays many parts,
His acts being seven ages.

Shakespeare compares the world (the tenor) to a theatrical stage (the vehicle) using a simple metaphor—but he does not stop there. He extends the idea/image present in the initial simple metaphor by enumerating the points of comparison further in the next few lines. Men and women are actors ('players') playing different roles ('parts'). Amidst birth ('entrances') and death ('exits'), man's life comprises seven ages ('acts'). An extended metaphor, such as this one, can therefore have additional tenors and vehicles. Here, 'men and women' is the secondary tenor; 'players', the secondary vehicle, and so on.

Emily Dickinson likens hope (tenor) to a bird (vehicle) using an extended metaphor in her poem 'Hope is the Thing with Feathers'. Can you spot the secondary tenor and vehicle in this metaphor?

> Hope is the thing with feathers
> That perches in the soul,
> And sings the tune

Other prominent examples of sustained metaphors may be seen in Walt Whitman's 'O Captain! My Captain!' (post-Civil War United States is compared to a ship that has survived a storm, thanks to her now-dead captain, the recently assassinated President Lincoln), and in T.S. Eliot's 'The Love Song of J. Alfred Prufrock' (the fog slowly enveloping a city is unforgettably compared to a cat).

Strained metaphor

A metaphor where the point of similarity is far-fetched is called a strained metaphor. See, for instance, this example from Shakespeare's *Macbeth*:

> Here lay Duncan,
> His silver skin laced with his golden blood

Duncan's blood (tenor), splattered on his skin, is compared to lace (vehicle). The resulting image of blood running across skin like a delicate pattern of decorative fabric, although vivid, is a bit too unusual and far-fetched.

The above line is also an example of a mixed metaphor. Can you find and explain the figure?

Guided exercise

Explain the nature of the analogy in the metphors given below. The tenor in each metaphor is indicated with a continuous underline, and the vehicle (where present), with a dotted underline.

1. The _waves_ thundered on the shore.
   Concentrate on the verb.

2. The _camel_ is the ship of the desert.
   Focus on the nouns.

3. I have measured out my _life_ with coffee spoons
   (Eliot, 'The Love Song of J. Alfred Prufrock')
   Concentrate on the verb: 'to measure out' means spending something carefully and in a restricted way.

4. The burnt-out ends of smoky _days_ (Eliot, 'Preludes')
   Interrogate the adjective.

5. _Variety_ is the spice of life.
   Focus on the nouns.

6. _Thy word_ is a lamp to my feet.
   Focus on the nouns.

7. _An aged man_ is but a paltry thing,
   A tattered coat upon a stick ... (Yeats, 'Sailing to Byzantium')
   An old man is compared to a scarecrow.

8. The ship ploughs the sea.
   Concentrate on the verb.

9. A dead _silence_ prevailed there.
   Interrogate the adjective.

10. And coming events cast their shadows before.
    (Campbell, 'Lochiel's Warning')
    Concentrate on the verb: a person casts his/her shadow.

11. _Thy wish_ was father ... to that thought.
    (Shakespeare, *Henry IV*, Part II)
    Focus on the nouns.

12. _Calamity_ / Is man's true touchstone.
    (Beaumont and Fletcher, *The Triumph of Honour*)
    Focus on the nouns.

13. I have no *spur* / To *prick the sides of my intent* ...
    (Shakespeare, *Macbeth*)
    A 'spur' is a sharp prod attached to a riding shoe, used to
    poke the sides of a slow horse to make it move faster. Macbeth
    compares his reluctant 'intent' (of killing Duncan) to a slow
    horse (the vehicle, which is not explicitly mentioned but
    understood through its association with 'spur').

14. *Life is* a *pilgrimage.*
    Focus on the nouns.

15. And *hope* is brightest when it *dawns* from fears.
    (Scott, *The Lady of the Lake*)
    Concentrate on the verb to figure out what hope is being
    compared to.

16. I should make very *forges of my cheeks*
    That would to cinders *burn up* modesty
    Did I but *speak* thy deeds. (Shakespeare, *Othello*)
    There are two connected metaphors here. Othello's cheeks are
    compared to a furnace ('forges'), and his speech to fire (this
    second vehicle is absent but can be identified through the verb
    'burn up').

17. But at my back I always hear
    Time's wingèd chariot hurrying near
    (Marvell, 'To His Coy Mistress')
    Focus on the nouns.

18. O listen! for the *Vale* profound
    Is *overflowing* with the sound.
    (Wordsworth, 'The Solitary Reaper')
    Concentrate on the verb 'overflowing'. The valley ('Vale'), filled
    up with music, is compared to an overflowing cup (the implied
    vehicle).

Figures based on Association

METONYMY

Derived from the Greek words *meta* (change) and *onoma* (name), metonymy literally means a 'change of name'. It is a figure of speech that substitutes/replaces a subject (the 'tenor') with a congruent/related image (the 'vehicle'), and solidifies the literal meaning.

In his *Manual of English Grammar and Composition*, John Nesfield defines metonymy as the 'describing [of] a thing by some accompaniment or significant adjunct, instead of naming the thing itself. When the sign is such as to strike the imagination more vividly that what it stands for, the language gains in impressiveness'. The thing meant (the actual subject) is substituted by a key image or a characteristic feature (its 'significant adjunct'). This image/characteristic is associated culturally with the subject. Let us examine a standard example of metonymy to see how it works.

The pen is mightier than the sword.

The meaning of this line is that the written word is more effective or influential than violence (or, alternatively, the writer is more powerful than the tyrant). The sentence carries two metonymical representations. The first one may be explained as follows.

- The thing mentioned, that is, the significant adjunct or image used: pen
- The thing meant, that is, the substituted subject: writing (or, a writer)
- The link between a pen and a writer/writing is external and cultural. Words can be written down through other implements as well. If the pen is taken away from the writer, he can use a pencil or charcoal. It is only culturally that a writer is associated with a pen (instead of pencil or charcoal).

In a similar way, the metonymy in the second part of the sentence can be examined as follows.

- The thing mentioned, that is, the significant adjunct or image used: sword
- The thing meant, that is, the substituted subject: violence (or, a tyrant—or anyone who relies heavily on oppression, or rules by means of the power of the sword)
- The link between a sword and a tyrant/violence is external and cultural. Violence can be perpetrated through weapons and means other than just a sword. If the sword is taken away from the tyrant, he can use machine guns or bombs. It is only culturally that a tyrant is associated with a sword.

The use of the images of a pen and a sword effectively solidifies the literal meaning that writing is more powerful than violence or oppressive state authorities. (That is why the latter often try to ban certain books that have a profound impact on public consciousness. Writers and books may be physically vulnerable, but tyrants are afraid of them.) We can see here that metonymy is a symbolising process.

Let us look at another example.

The press criticised the White House.

The images present in the line are 'the press' (printing machine) and 'the White House'. The images are obviously being used figuratively, since a printing machine cannot literally criticise a building. The things mentioned ('press', 'White House') are merely substitutes for the actual subjects (to which they are connected culturally). 'The press' represents journalists working in newspapers, and, by extension, media persons working for television. The 'White House' stands for not only the office of the US president, but also the executive branch of the US government.

Let us now consider Shelley's 'Song to the Men of England' which deftly analyses the contemporary political situation by using two major tropes—metaphor and metonymy—together, and defers the literal meaning by using comparison and substitution. The bee metaphor should be obvious if you have gone through the chapter on metaphor. The second line below contains two examples of metonymical substitution.

> Wherefore feed, and clothe, and save,
> From the cradle to the grave,
> Those ungrateful drones who would
> Drain your sweat—nay, drink your blood?

'The cradle' and 'the grave' are two concrete images that replace 'birth' and 'death' respectively, two abstract states of being.

In Shakespeare's comedy *Twelfth Night*, Lady Olivia's 'sweet Roman hand' metonymically refers to her beautiful handwriting. There is a deferral of literal meaning as 'handwriting' is substituted by the image of 'hand'.

There has been a debate on the nature of the association in metonymy: whether it is intrinsic or not. Most recent theorists stress that all figurative representations are arbitrary and culture-specific, and that there is no intrinsic association between the tenor (the subject) and the vehicle (the image). Take, for example, Keats's poem 'On Receiving a Laurel Crown from Leigh Hunt', which contrasts the wreath of laurel twigs with turbans and crowns. In the lines that follow, he places the glorious poet far above emperors and kings.

> Two bending laurel Sprigs 'tis nearly pain
> To be conscious of such a Coronet.
> Still time is fleeting, and no dream arises
> Gorgeous as I would have it only I see
> A Trampling down of what the world most prizes
> Turbans and Crowns, and blank regality;

If we make a wreath with laurel twigs and place it ceremoniously on an Indian's head, he might not know what to make to make of it. However, in Western culture, a laurel coronet stands for victory and glory. We see that the link between the thing named (that is, the laurel crown) and the thing meant (that is, poetic glory) is external and cultural. In the similar way, 'turbans and crowns' metonymically represent (Oriental) emperors and (Western) monarchs.

There may be nine different kinds of metonymic substitution. You can use the mnemonic **MISCAPE** to remember these varieties.

M (1) The **maker** for her/his work, and
     (2) the **place** for its production
I (3) The **instrument** or organ for the agent
S (4) The **symbol** or sign for the thing symbolised
C (5) The **container** for the thing contained
A (6) The **act** for its object
P (7) The name of a **passion** for the object inspiring it
E (8) The **effect** for the cause, or (9) the **cause** for the effect

Guided exercise

Explain the figure of speech in the lines given below. The examples of metonymy have been grouped by type to guide you, and further hints have been provided in brackets, where required.

The **maker** for her/his work, and the **place** for its production

1. He is weak in *Euclid*. (geometry by Euclid)
2. We read *Tagore*. (works of Rabindranath Tagore)
3. And all *Arabia* breathes from yonder box.
   (perfumes from Arabia)
4. O for a beaker full of the warm *South*
   (wine from southern France)

The student will do well to remember the names of some places known for their products; for example, *China* for ceramic ware; *Morocco* for leather; *Champagne* for wines; *Havana* for cigars; and so on.

The **instrument** or organ for the agent

5. And mighty *hearts* are held in slender chains. (the heroine Belinda's male admirers)
6. Give every man thine *ear*, but few thy *voice*. (listen to everyone; say little yourself)
7. He is a good *hand* at composition. (talent, flair)
8. They carried *fire and sword* into the country.
   (a devastating war)
9. The *tongue* of slander is never silent.
   (people who malign others)

The **symbol** or sign for the thing symbolised

10. He ascended the *throne*. (sovereignty)
11. She was raised to *the bench*. (judgeship)
12. *Sceptre* and *crown* must tumble down.
    (monarchy, royal power)
13. *Grey hairs* should be respected. (old age)
14. Urgent development work is often delayed due to *red tape*.
    (official procedure)
15. One must show deference to *the chair*. (the chairman)
16. The star's personal jewellery was brought to *the hammer* at
    Sotheby's. (put up for auction)
17. He got the issue fixed using *backstairs* influence.
    (secret, improper)
18. She was called to *the bar*. (made a barrister)

The **container** for the thing contained

19. All the *world* knows him. (people of the world)
20. He drank the poisoned *cup*. (contents of the cup)
21. He keeps a sumptuous *table*. (food on the table)
22. Who steals my *purse*, steals trash. (contents of my purse)
23. The entire *auditorium* laughed. (audience)
24. He is too fond of the *bottle*. (alcohol)
25. The *kettle* boils. (water in the kettle)
26. The conquerors smote the *city*. (inhabitants of the city)
27. To go over to *Rome* (Catholicism, which is centred in Rome)
28. He keeps a fine *stable*. (fine horses)
29. The *gallery* applauded loudly. (spectators in the gallery)
30. *India* does not desire war with *Pakistan*. (Indians, Pakistanis)

The **act** for its object

31. The principles of democracy were the *scoff* of the imperialists.
    (object of ridicule)
32. The people's *prayer*, the glad diviner's *theme*, the young men's
    vision, and the old men's *dream*. (object of devotion, etc.)

The name of a **passion** for the object inspiring it

33. Gandhiji is the *pride* of India.
34. The boy is the *sigh* of the rising family.
35. The applause, *delight*, the *wonder* of our stage!
    My Shakespeare, rise.

36. She is coming, my *life*, my *fate*
37. For Lycidas, your *sorrow*, is not dead.

The **effect** for the cause, or **cause** for the effect

38. Swiftly flies the feathered *death*. (arrow, causing death)
39. The bright *death* quivered at the victim's throat. (shining sword, causing death)
40. With sorrow and suffering came early *grey hairs*. (old age, causing grey hair)

SYNECDOCHE

Derived from the Greek word for 'receiving together' or 'shared understanding', synecdoche can be seen as a special case of the substitution of a subject (the tenor) with an image (the vehicle) which is not only congruent or intimately related to it but also inseparable from it.

This usually takes two opposite forms: substitution of a part for the whole, or the whole for a part. Synecdoche may be seen as a special form of metonymy. Let us see a few examples. The first is from Milton's *Paradise Lost*:

> Will ye submit your necks, and choose to bend
> The supple knee?

In the above lines, Satan asks his followers whether they are going to yield to God's command. 'Necks' and 'knees' stand for whole persons of the fallen angels.

> All hands on deck!

Here, 'hands' (the image) replaces and represents 'the sailors working on a ship' (the subject). Notice that hands are the most needed body part of these workers: they are needed to manipulate the ship, set up sails, clean the deck, etc. Otherwise, the captain would have ordered, say, all 'faces' to appear on deck. However, 'face' can also stand for a person when it is the most important part, as we can see in the following example from Shakespeare's *Macbeth*:

> Take thy face hence.

The servant who came to inform Macbeth of the arrival of the English force was trembling with fear. He had a pale face, which indicates emotional distress. Macbeth orders the boy out of the room as he did not wish to see his followers afraid of the enemy.

Similarly, a specific instance of a class can be used to refer to a general type or the class as a whole.

> India's Shakespeare wrote in Sanskrit.
> The American Gandhi was assassinated in 1968.

In the above examples, an image/vehicle ('India's Shakespeare', 'American Gandhi') is substituted for the actual subject/tenor (Kalidasa and Martin Luther King Jr, respectively). The substitution uses a specific instance of a general class (Shakespeare, an exemplar of a great dramatist; Gandhi, an exemplar of someone who fights nonviolently for a just cause) to both represent and illuminate the subject. Archetypes, mythic characters, gods and goddesses have all been viewed as synecdochical, as have some literary characters, such as Hamlet, Macbeth, Othello, Desdemona, Romeo, Juliet, Jane Eyre, and Willy Loman.

The eight varieties of synecdochical substitution may be remembered by using the mnemonic SAPIM. Note that some letters stand for two types of substitution.

S   (1) The **species** for the genus
(a specific thing for a more general one), and
(2) the **genus** for the species
(a general thing for a more specific one)
A   (3) The **abstract** for the concrete, and
(4) the **concrete** for the abstract
P   (5) The **part** for the whole, and (6) the **whole** for the part
I   (7) The **individual** for the class (antonomasia)
M   (8) The **material** for the thing made of it

Synecdoche, therefore, substitutes one entity for another which is (1) directly/intimately connected to it, and is (2) either a more general or a more specific/individual avatar of it.

Metonymy and synecdoche

Many critics consider synecdoche to be a special type of metonymy. In both metonymy and synecdoche, the tenor is associated in some way to the vehicle. However, there is a slight difference. In synecdoche, the two associated things are practically identical, and the connection between them is inseparable and internal. In metonymy, they are different from each other, and the connection between them is in thought alone; the associated things are separable, and one is external to the other.

Shakespeare deftly uses metonymy and synecdoche together in the following line from *Henry IV, Part 2*:

Uneasy lies the head that wears a crown.

Exhausted, sick and troubled by uprisings, King Henry IV spends sleepless nights. The 'head' is an example of synecdoche (a part for the whole, that is, the person). A 'crown', on the other hand, metonymically represents the responsibilities of a king (sign or symbol for the thing symbolised, that is, monarchy). Applied together, the figures in the line mean 'the one who rules will always have troubles and worries'.

Guided exercise

Explain the figure of speech in the lines given below. The examples of synecdoche have been grouped by type to guide you, and further hints have been provided in brackets.

The **species** for the genus

1. To earn one's *bread* (food)
2. *Silver and gold* have I none. (money)
3. No, rather I abjure all *roofs*, and choose (shelter)
   To be a comrade with the *wolf and owl* (animals)

The **genus** for the species

4. He is a poor *creature*. (man)
5. Would you like a *drink*? (alcoholic drink)
6. The *vessel* ran aground. (ship)
7. The soldiers saw *action* at the border. (battle)
8. A wretched *individual* (man)

A broad, general term is often substituted for a more particular word that we might not wish or like to mention, as seen in the lines below.

9. Mrs Malden was a *plain* woman. (ugly)
10. I dedicate this book to my dear, *departed* friend. (dead)
11. They read the will of the *deceased*. (dead)

12. The insurance scheme will provide for your family in case *anything* should happen to you. (death)

The **abstract** for the concrete
An abstract noun is used as a common noun.

13. Let not *Ambition* mock their useful toil. (ambitious men)
14. All the *rank and fashion* came out to see the sight. (men of position and of fashion)
15. Lowliness is young *ambition's* ladder. (ambitious men)
16. *Ambition* should be made of sterner stuff. (ambitious men)
17. I am out of *humanity's* reach. (humankind)

The **concrete** for the abstract
A common noun denoting a person is used in an abstract sense.

18. There is a mixture of *the tiger and the ape* in the character of a Frenchman. (animal instincts)
19. The *father* in the judge forgave the boy-criminal. (fatherly feelings)
20. The sleeping *mother* awoke in her at the sight of the dead child. (motherly feelings)
21. I hate *the viceroy*, love the man. (the viceroyalty and its attendant powers)

The **part** for the whole

22. Three *summers* I have lived there. (years)
23. All *hands* are on strike. (workers)
24. A girl of sixteen *summers* (years)
25. A *sail* was spotted in the distance. (ship)
26. An old man of eighty *winters* (years)
27. Perhaps in this neglected spot is laid
    Some *heart* once pregnant with celestial fire (person)
    Hands, that the rod of empire might have swayed (men)

The **whole** for the part

28. The smiling *year* (spring)
29. The falling *year* (autumn)
30. The lavish moisture of the melting *year* (rainy season)
31. *West Indies* won the test match. (the West Indian national cricket team)

An **individual** for the class

A proper noun is used as a common noun. Such a figure of speech is also known as **antonomasia**.

32. A *Daniel* come to judgement (a wise, impartial judge)
33. Some mute inglorious *Milton* here may rest, (a great poet)
    Some *Cromwell* guiltless of his country's blood.
    (a great revolutionary)
34. He is a *Judas*. (a traitor)
35. The days of *Gandhi* are no more. (noble men)
36. Every Bengali novelist is not a *Saratchandra*. (great novelist)
37. He is a *Shylock*. (moneylender)

The **material** for the thing made of it

38. Since *brass*, nor *stone*, nor earth, nor boundless sea / But sad mortality o'er-sways their power (imposing sculptures/ structures made of brass and stone)
39. In that rich earth a richer *dust* concealed. (body)
40. Look at the *stone* where my dead father lies. (tomb)
41. He is dressed in *linen*. (linen clothes)
42. The prisoner was bound in *irons*. (chains)

Common examples of this type of synecdoche include: 'brass' for brass instruments, sculptures, or the shell casings of bullet cartridges; 'cement' for concrete (cement being just the binder in concrete); 'glasses' for spectacles; 'plastic' for a credit card; 'steel' for a sword; 'tin' for a container with tin plating.

Transferred Epithet (Hypallage)

An 'epithet' is an adverb or an adjective (or a phrase including either) which modifies a noun. The transferred epithet is a figure of speech wherein an adverb or adjective is transferred from a noun to which it properly belongs, to a noun with which it fits grammatically but not logically.

Also known as hypallage (derived from the Greek word for 'interchange' or 'exchange'), a transferred epithet involves shifting a modifier from one noun to another, changing the structure of a sentence and reinforcing its literal meaning.

His coward lips did from their colour fly.
(Shakespeare, *Julius Caesar*)

The adjective 'coward' should have qualified the person being referred to. Instead, his lips are attributed this quality: they have turned pale as the person is unnerved.

Guided exercise

Explain the figure of speech in the lines given below. Remember: an epithet is an adjective.

1. He was engaged in a *dishonest calling*.
2. The ploughman homeward plods his *weary way*
   (Gray, 'Elegy Written in a Country Churchyard')
3. Three *sleepless nights* I passed ... (Wordsworth, *The Borderers*)
4. When I am dead, my dearest, / Sing no *sad songs* for me
   (Rossetti, 'Song')
5. Brushing with *hasty steps* the dews away
   (Gray, 'Elegy Written in a Country Churchyard')
6. Children ardent for some *desperate glory*
   (Owen, 'Dulce Et Decorum Est')
7. Some *pious drops* the closing eye requires
   (Gray, 'Elegy Written in a Country Churchyard')

There are several examples of hypallage in popular parlance, such as: 'a virtuous indignation', 'a happy thought', 'an unlucky remark', etc.

ALLUSION

An allusion is a brief, indirect reference to a presumably familiar person, event, statement, or theme found in art and literature, myth and history, religion and culture. As a figure of speech, it enriches meaning by adding layers of association beyond its literal meaning. Consider the following passage from Shakespeare's *Twelfth Night*:

> O, when mine eyes did see Olivia first, ...
> That instant was I turn'd into a hart;
> And my desires, like fell and cruel hounds,
> E'er since pursue me.

The above lines are spoken by Orsino, who is infatuated with Olivia. The lines contain an indirect reference, an allusion, to the classical myth of the moon-goddess Diana and the shepherd Actaeon. Diana, incensed by Actaeon peeping at her while she was bathing, turned him into a stag. He ended up being killed by his own hounds. Just like Actaeon, Orsino is hunted down by his own passions. This mythical allusion enriches Orsino's story by adding layers of signification.

Such connotations can be understood or appreciated by a large audience if the reference is to myth and religion or to popular culture. However, some poets and playwrights create densely allusive works that demand from the reader erudition in various fields of culture. T.S. Eliot's *The Waste Land* (1922) is a famous example of densely allusive writing. In the 434-line poem, Eliot alludes to the work of a long list of authors including Homer, Sophocles, Virgil, Dante, Chaucer, Shakespeare, Milton, Wagner, Whitman, Baudelaire, Verlaine and Conrad, in addition to making extensive use of scriptural writings (such as the *Brihadaranyaka Upanishad*, the Buddha's *Fire Sermon*, and the *Book of Common Prayer*) as well as cultural and anthropological studies (primarily James Frazer's *The Golden Bough* and Jessie Weston's *From Ritual to Romance*).

Guided exercise

Explain the figure of speech in the lines given below.

1. But thy eternal summer shall not fade,
    Nor lose possession of that fair thou ow'st,
    Nor shall death brag thou wander'st in his *shade*
    (Shakespeare, 'Sonnet 18')
    The reference to 'shade' is an allusion to Psalm 23.

2. All night the *dreadless Angel* unpursu'd
    Through Heav'ns wide Champain held his way, till Morn,
    Wak't by the *circling Hours, with rosie hand*
    Unbarr'd the gates of Light. (Milton, *Paradise Lost*)
    In these lines, we count no fewer than three allusions: one to Abdiel, one to the Greek myth of the Horae, and one to Homer's *The Odyssey*.

3. Another age shall see the golden ear
    Embrown the slope, and nod on the parterre,
    Deep harvests bury all his pride has plann'd,
    And laughing *Ceres* reassume the land.
    (Pope, *Epistles to Several Persons*)

Here Pope alludes to Demeter, the goddess of wheat and grain, showing how this place will once again return to earth for plough.

4. Sylvan historian, who canst thus express
   A flowery tale more sweetly than our rhyme:
   What leaf-fringed legend haunts about thy shape
   Of deities or mortals, or of both,
   In *Tempe* or the dales of Arcady?
   (Keats, 'Ode on a Grecian Urn')

   'Tempe' is an allusion to the Vale of Tempe, a region in Greece so beautiful that Apollo and the Muses were believed to visit it frequently.

5. All overgrown by cunning moss,
   All interspersed with weed,
   The little cage of '*Currer Bell*'
   In quiet '*Haworth*' laid.
   (Dickinson, 'All Overgrown by Cunning Moss')

   The italicised words are allusions to the writer Charlotte Brontë, who used Currer Bell as a pen name, and to her native village.

Literary allusion is closely related to parody and pastiche, which are also literary devices involving references to other texts. Burlesque, charade, and lampoon are different types of parody that mimic another text's style or content for a comic or satirical effect. Pastiche, a term familiar in postmodernism, refers to open and intentional borrowing from or imitation of an earlier style. Carl Sandburg's poetry is often a conscious and open pastiche of Walt Whitman's work.

Figures based on Difference or Contrast

ANTITHESIS

A 'thesis' is a premise, a proposition; that is, an unproven assumption that is put forward. The term comes from the Greek word for 'something put forth', and refers to a statement which needs to be defended by the speaker. In political speech, as well as in everyday conversation, a powerful device to defend your thesis is the use of antithesis.

An 'antithesis' is an explicit statement that juxtaposes implicitly contrasted ideas. Derived from a Greek word signifying 'set against', the antithesis is a rhetorical device by which two diametrically contrasting ideas are set against one another in a parallel and balanced form for emphasis.

A century before Derrida and the poststructuralists, John Nesfield drew the reader's attention to the fact that language works in binaries of concepts such as light/dark, black/white, man/woman, and so on, and words depend on other words for signification:

> We cannot use the commonest word, say 'weak' for example, without inwardly contrasting it with 'strong'. Barring proper names, which are mere marks or tokens, and interjections, which are mere sounds, there is not a word in our language, or in fact in any language, which does not imply some other word or words with which it is contrasted in meaning. This law is so universal, that in ordinary speech it is sufficient to mention one word, such as 'weak', without adding its negative form 'not strong'. (*Manual of English Grammar and Composition*)

Antithesis exploits this disposition of language in order to powerfully drive home the orator's point. As Aristotle pointed out, 'Such a form of speech is *satisfying*, because the significance of contrasted ideas is easily felt, especially when they are thus put side by side' (*Rhetoric*, italics added).

An excellent example of antithesis used in political speech is a line attributed to the eighteenth-century American revolutionary Patrick Henry:

> Give me liberty, or give me death!

Gandhi's 'Karenge ya marenge' is its Asiatic counterpart. The following exhortation by Martin Luther King Jr deserves mention:

> We must learn to live together as brothers or perish together as fools.

Here is an example from Milton's *Paradise Lost*:

> Better to reign in Hell than serve in Heaven.

We have to note that antithesis depends on correct syntax and patterns of sentences. Let us see how these lines work.

> Give me liberty, or give me death!
> We must learn to live together as brothers or perish together as fools.
> Better to reign in Hell than serve in Heaven.

All three statements are fine examples of political persuasion directed at a colonised, oppressed or defeated people. And all of them depend on their syntax for their effect. These statements lose their urgency and power if their second halves are chopped off. 'Give me liberty!', 'Learn to live together as brothers' or 'Dear comrades, it is fine to reign in Hell!' sound not only incomplete but also unconvincing. These statements benefit greatly in terms of rhetorical power if one adds opposite statements to them in a matching form. Juxtaposing parts that are formally different—for example, 'Give me liberty; otherwise you can consider sending me to the gallows'—will not work. To give power to an idea, we need to

- balance it with an opposite or contrasting idea
- match the form of both ideas

In the above examples, *liberty*, *co-existence* and *sovereignty* strike a balance with *death*, *destruction* and *servitude* respectively.

Antithesis is, therefore, a rhetorical device that can transform a plainly worded idea into a powerful appeal, as evidenced by the examples below.

United we stand, divided we fall.

- The idea, in plain words: unity is power.
- The idea is expressed powerfully through the juxtaposition of two opposite/contrasting ideas.
- The juxtaposed phrases are balanced by matching their forms: *united* balances with *divided*; *stand* balances with *fall*.

God made the country, and man made the town. (William Cowper, *The Task*)

- The idea, in plain words: man has failed to conserve nature.
- The idea is expressed powerfully through the juxtaposition of two opposite/contrasting ideas.
- The juxtaposed phrases are balanced by matching their forms: *God* balances with *man*; *country* balances with *town*.

Guided exercise

Explain the nature of the contrast in the lines given below. The contrasting entities are indicated using continuous and dotted underlining.

1. Crabbed age and youth cannot live together:
    Youth is full of pleasure, *age is full of care*;
    Youth like summer morn, *age like winter weather*;
    Youth like summer brave, *age like winter bare*.
    Youth is full of sport, *age's breath is short*;
    Youth is nimble, *age is lame*;
    Youth is hot and bold, *age is weak and cold*;
    Youth is wild, and *age is tame*.
    Age, I do abhor thee, *youth, I do adore thee*;
    O! my love, my love is young:
    Age, I do defy thee: O! sweet shepherd, hie thee,
    For methinks thou stay'st too long. (attributed to Shakespeare)

2. *To be*, or *not to be*, that is the question—
    Whether 'tis nobler in the mind *to suffer*
    The slings and arrows of outrageous fortune,

Or *to take arms against a sea of troubles*,
And by opposing, end them? (Shakespeare, *Hamlet*)

3. *He works his work, I mine*. (Tennyson, 'Ulysses')

4. The *evil* that men do *lives* after them. The *good* is *oft interred* with their bones. (Shakespeare, *Julius Caesar*)

5. *On one side stands modesty, on the other impudence*; on one, *fidelity*, on the other, *deceit*; here, *piety*, there, *sacrilege*; here, *continency*, there, *lust* ... (Cicero, 'Catiline Oration' II)

6. *To err is human, to forgive divine*. (Pope, *An Essay on Criticism*)

7. *Not that I loved Caesar less*, but that *I loved Rome more*. (Shakespeare, *Julius Caesar*)

8. A *man's face is his autobiography*. A *woman's face is her work of fiction*. (Wilde)

9. *Man proposes, God disposes*.
(Thomas à Kempis, *The Imitation of Christ*)

10. The *prodigal robs his heir*, the *miser robs himself*.
(Jean de La Bruyère, *Characters*)

11. *Charms strike the sight*, but *merit wins the soul*.
(Pope, *The Rape of the Lock*)

12. For *evil news rides post*, while *good news baits*.
(Milton, *Samson Agonistes*)

13. ... *love th' offender*, yet *detest th' offence* (Pope, *Eloisa to Abelard*)

14. Love *sought is good*, but *given unsought better*.
(Shakespeare, *Twelfth Night*)

15. *Heard melodies are sweet*, but *those unheard / Are sweeter* ...
(Keats, 'Ode on a Grecian Urn')

EPIGRAM

The term 'epigram' comes from the Greek word for 'inscription', brief poems engraved on tombstones or monuments, or on offerings to the gods. In the domain of rhetoric, epigram is a brief and witty statement marked by a strong element of surprise. It is characterised by an apparent contradiction in language which causes a temporary shock, but a little reflection discloses a deeper meaning. The beauty of an epigram lies in its brevity, universality of meaning, and apparent contradiction in language. As Coleridge summarises aptly,

> What is an epigram? A dwarfish whole;
> Its body brevity, and wit its soul.

Coleridge here alludes to Shakespeare's remark that brevity is the soul of wit: an epigram is remarkably short, but bristling with a lively wit.

Consider the following example from Edmund Burke's *Reflections on the Revolution in France*:

> Our antagonist is our helper.

- Apparent contradiction: How can an antagonist (enemy) be a helper (friend)? This contradiction causes a temporary shock.
- Deeper meaning: When we reflect on this further, we realise that an enemy helps us correct our faults by pointing out our weaknesses. In this sense, an enemy is an ally.

The concluding couplet of Shakespeare's 'Sonnet 76' is an epigram:

> For as the sun is daily new and old,
> So is my love still telling what is told.

- Apparent contradiction: The sun and the poet's love are, surprisingly, both old and new.
- Deeper meaning: Both constantly renew themselves.

The following witticism is attributed to the French diplomat Charles Maurice de Talleyrand-Périgord:

> Speech was given to man to conceal his thoughts.

- Apparent contradiction: It is common knowledge that speech is used to express one's thoughts.
- Deeper meaning: Most of the time, it is not possible to speak one's mind. One has to be diplomatic and careful about what one says. Even when one is speaking his mind, he has to choose his words carefully to avoid trouble.

Alexander Pope frequently uses epigrams in his writings, often with a satirical edge. *An Essay on Criticism* (1711), for example, features many epigrams that have become well-known expressions in our day. For example, the following contemptuous line directed towards the literary critics of his day has become a common proverb:

> ... fools rush in where angels fear to tread.

- Apparent contradiction: Simpletons foraying into an area cautiously avoided by insightful people seems a strange idea.
- Deeper meaning: Immature people often try to deal with or talk about a profoundly important matter without being qualified to do so.

The epigram was a favourite device of not just eighteenth-century poetry: the Romantic poets found in its compactness a vehicle for the sublime. Consider the following lines from Blake's 'Auguries of Innocence':

> To see a World in a Grain of Sand
> And a Heaven in a Wild Flower,
> Hold Infinity in the palm of your hand,
> And Eternity in an hour.

In each of the four lines, the reader finds statements that are surprising at first but have profound meanings which come out on close reading. It is proposed that the infinitesimal can contain infinity. This idea may seem literally impossible but reveals a spiritual truth.

The fin-de-siècle playwright Oscar Wilde is famous for his subversive epigrams:

> The only way to get rid of a temptation is to yield to it.
> Whenever people agree with me, I always feel that I must be wrong.
> Consistency is the last refuge of the unimaginative.
> The truth is rarely pure and never simple.
> Seriousness is the only refuge of the shallow.

See also **paradox**, page 63.

Antithesis and epigram

Let us see the difference between an antithesis and an epigram by examining an example of each.

> Man is a hater of truth, a lover of fiction. (Landor) ANTITHESIS
> My only love sprung from my only hate! (Shakespeare) EPIGRAM

- Antithesis relies on *true* contradiction. A 'hater of truth' is a 'lover of fiction': this is self-explanatory and the statement does not strike the reader as unusual. In an epigram, the contradiction is *apparent*: the idea of love springing from hate strikes one as unusual.
- The epigram has a *hidden meaning*; but in antithesis, the meaning is *clearly defined* by ruling out the opposite.
- The antithesis can be recognised by its peculiar syntax and balanced arrangement: 'hater of truth' is in a balanced juxtaposition with 'lover of fiction'. An epigram is recognised by its brevity and wit, that is, by its ingenious use of language.

Antithetical statements may have an epigrammatic force, but the key to recognising them lies in their structure.

Guided exercise

Explain the figure of speech in the lines given below. Note their proverbial quality and try to find out their deeper meaning. Key words that highlight the apparent contradictions are italicised.

1. Some cause happiness *wherever* they go; others *whenever* they go. (attributed to Wilde)

   The second instance of 'go' in this funny statement means 'leave' or 'depart'. Everyone present is relieved when these people go away.

2. Bigotry is the *sacred disease*. (Heraclitus, 'Fragment 46')

3. Those who *cannot remember the past* are condemned to *repeat it*. (George Santayana, *The Life of Reason*)

4. Our sincerest *laughter*
   With some *pain* is fraught (Shelley, 'To a Skylark')

5. Our *sweetest songs* are those that tell of *saddest thought*. (Shelley, 'To a Skylark')

   Sorrow moves the heart towards sympathy, a nobler feeling than happiness. Sad songs are, therefore, closer to our hearts.

6. *Failures* are the *pillars of success*.

7. Cowards *die many times before* their *deaths*. (Shakespeare, *Julius Caesar*)

   It is impossible to 'die' before one's death. However, 'die' in the above statement means being afflicted by the fear of death.

8. *Hypocrisy* is the *homage* that vice pays to virtue.
   (La Rochefoucauld, *Maximes*)

9. *Art* lies in *concealing art.*

   In the first instance, 'art' means 'works that are recognised as art'; the second use of the word 'art' stands for 'artistry' or 'technique'. Successful art is effortlessly beautiful—it does not highlight technical mastery.

10. The *Child* is *father of* the *Man.*
    (Wordsworth, 'My Heart Leaps Up')

    It is biologically impossible for a child to be the father of an adult. 'Father' here means a guide who can teach an adult to tear the veil of familiarity and look at nature with childlike wonder.

11. Beware the *fury* of a *patient* man.
    (Dryden, *Absalom and Achitophel*)

12. The paths of *glory* lead but to the *grave.*
    (Gray, 'Elegy Written in a Country Churchyard')

    Glory is considered eternal but is ephemeral in actuality. 'Grave' stands for not only death but also oblivion.

13. ... *facts* are a very inferior form of *fiction.*
    (Woolf, 'How Should One Read a Book?')

    What we call 'facts' are merely dry details, shorn of the vividness and intensity of life captured by fiction.

14. *Sweet* are the uses of *adversity.* (Shakespeare, *As You Like It*)

15. In my *beginning* is my *end.* (Eliot, 'East Coker')

16. He makes no *friend* who never made a *foe.*
    (Tennyson, *Idylls of the King*)

17. He is *all fault* who hath *no fault* at all
    (Tennyson, *Idylls of the King*)

18. To be prepared for *war* is one of the most effectual means of preserving *peace.* (Washington, 'Address to Congress')

19. No one ever *teaches well* who *wants to teach*, or *governs well* who *wants to govern* ...
    (Ruskin quoting Plato, *The Crown of Wild Olive*)

A teacher's job is to help students learn, not put himself on a pedestal. A ruler's job is to govern, not seek power. Pursuit of the latter goals usually leads to neglect of original responsibilities.

20. ... *bless* the hand that gave the *blow*.
(Dryden, *The Spanish Friar*)

21. *Excess of ceremony* shows *want of breeding*.

22. More *haste*, less *speed*.

23. They also *serve* who only *stand and wait*.
(Milton, 'On His Blindness')

24. *Silence* is sometimes more eloquent than *words*.

25. I must be *cruel*, only to be *kind*. (Shakespeare, *Hamlet*)

OXYMORON

An extreme form of epigram, the oxymoron juxtaposes two apparently contradictory words. 'Oxymoron' is derived from the Greek words *oksús* ('sharp' or 'pointed') and *mōros* ('dull' or 'foolish'), and is thus itself an oxymoron: 'pointedly dull'.

An element of deeper truth always justifies such juxtapositions. This relates to how writers use this device. Oxymorons are often inserted to highlight absurdities, or to explain complicated or intense feelings—so complicated that they can only be explained by words that do not make sense.

Let us consider an example from Owen's 'The Send-off'.

And lined the train with faces grimly gay.

- Juxtaposition of two contrasting words: 'grim' and 'gay'
- Apparent contradiction: A person can hardly be dour-spirited ('grim') and cheerful ('gay') at the same time. The juxtaposition seems untenable.
- Inner meaning: The departing soldiers put on a brave and cheerful face, but are apprehensive of death at the battle front.
- The expression has an element of epigrammatic brevity.

Let us consider another example of oxymoron, from Wordsworth's 'The World Is Too Much With Us':

> Little we see in Nature that is ours;
> We have given our hearts away, a sordid boon!

- Juxtaposition of two contrasting words: 'sordid' and 'boon'
- Apparent contradiction: A blessing ('boon') cannot be 'sordid', that is, shorn of beauty and morality. The juxtaposition seems untenable.
- Inner meaning: Modernity is a mixed blessing. It has benefitted us, but also degraded our minds and souls.
- The expression has an element of epigrammatic brevity.

No one would deny that modernity has blessed our lives in myriad ways: giving up the benefits of science and technology and returning to an earlier time does not make sense. Still, separated from nature, modern man has lost humane values such as mercy, pity, peace and love.

The line given below, from Tennyson's *Idylls of the King*, contains two oxymorons:

> And faith unfaithful kept him falsely true.

The following extract from Shakespeare's *Romeo and Juliet* features a series of oxymorons:

> Why then, O brawling love! O loving hate!
> O anything of nothing first created!
> O heavy lightness, serious vanity,
> Misshapen chaos of well-seeming forms!
> Feather of lead, bright smoke, cold fire, sick health,
> Still-waking sleep, that is not what it is!
> This love feel I, that feel no love in this.

Such oxymorons, used to express the unique agony of the courtly lover, comprise the stock rhetoric of the Petrarchan tradition of love poetry.

The most common form of oxymoron involves an ill-matching adjective–noun combination which presents a seemingly odd idea. Common examples of oxymorons include 'white lies', 'open secret', 'pious fraud', 'noble revenge', 'tedious amusement', and 'silent rebuke'. Noun–verb combinations, as well as noun–noun combinations, are also seen sometimes.

Oxymoron and epigram

Both epigram and oxymoron rely on striking contradictions that might seem meaningless at first glance. However, the reader soon realises that the apparent contradiction is only an example of innovative language use. The writer is trying to convey a complex meaning that cannot be expressed in literal terms.

The formal peculiarity of the oxymoron differentiates it from the epigram; that is, the difference between the two is that of structure. Whereas in an oxymoron the contradictory words are placed side by side, in an epigram the words are set at a distance. It is often said that the oxymoron is an extreme case of the epigram.

Guided exercise

Explain the figure of speech in the lines below. The contradictory words are italicised for you.

1. He is the most *learned fool* in the country.

2. Thus *idly busy* rolls their world away. (Goldsmith, *The Traveller*)

3. With *wanton heed*, and *giddy cunning* (Milton, *L'Allegro*)

4. ... whose dread command / Is *lawless law*
   (Byron, *Childe Harold's Pilgrimage*)

5. The *bookful blockhead*, ignorantly read
   (Pope, *An Essay on Criticism*)

6. ... yet from whose flames
   No light, but rather *darkness visible*
   Served only to discover sights of woe (Milton, *Paradise Lost*)

7. This *pleasing anxious* being ...
   (Gray, 'Elegy Written in a Country Churchyard')

8. Such *harmonious madness*
   From my lips would flow ... (Shelley, 'To a Skylark')

9. Thou *pure impiety* and *impious purity*.
   (Shakespeare, *Much Ado About Nothing*)

10. Forgiveness is the *noblest revenge.*

CLIMAX

This figure consists in ascending degrees of verbal power and rhetorical importance as a sentence progresses. In climax (derived from the Greek word for 'ladder'), words, ideas or sentiments are stated in such a manner that the meaning rises from a less important or impressive stage to a more important or impressive one. Ideas are arranged in ascending order of importance so that each succeeding idea is more striking and impressive than the previous one. Look at the following example from Tennyson's 'Ulysses':

> To strive, to seek, to find, and not to yield.

There are two ways to create a climax.

1. Z<Y<X: As a candidate, Mr Roy is good, but Mr Ahmed is better, and Mr Sen is surely the best!
2. X>Y>Z: Mr Sen may not be the most perfect candidate, but Mr Ahmed is worse, and Mr Roy is the worst.

In the first case, we climb up the ladder, and in the second, we sit at the highest step and look downwards. In either of these arrangements, the effect is positive: both sentences create a favourable impression about Mr Sen. We do not descend the stairs to a letdown, as it happens in **anticlimax** (page 58).

The student should note that we are dealing with climax as a *stylistic device*, which deals with the arrangement of words, phrases, or clauses; and not with 'climax' as a certain point of heightened tension in a dramatic narrative. For climax as a narrative element, look up 'Freytag's pyramid' to understand how tension is built and resolved in a narrative.

Guided exercise

Explain the figure of speech in the lines given below. The keywords are italicised.

1. I *came*, I *saw*, I *conquered*. (attributed to Julius Caesar)

   The highlighted actions follow an ascending order of seriousness.

   See also **asyndeton**, page 118.

2. ... a heart to *resolve*, a head to *contrive*, and a hand to *execute* (Gibbon, *Decline and Fall of the Roman Empire*)

   To pledge, to plan, and to perform are actions that follow an ascending order of seriousness.

3. How *noble* in reason, how *infinite* in faculty! ... In action how *like an angel*, in apprehension how *like a god*! (Shakespeare, *Hamlet*)

   The epithets used to praise Man increase in magnitude from 'noble' to 'infinite' to 'angelic' to 'godlike'.

4. Some books are to be *tasted*, others to be *swallowed*, and some few to be *chewed and digested*. (Bacon, 'Of Studies')

   Bacon says that some books need only be browsed through, some read quickly for entertainment, while some others invite close reading. These ideas follow an ascending order of rhetorical impact.

5. *Reading* maketh a *full* man; *conference* a *ready* man; and *writing* an *exact* man. (Bacon, 'Of Studies')

   The activities of 'reading', 'conference' and 'writing'—as well as the attributes fullness, readiness and exactitude—follow an ascending order of seriousness.

6. The *port is near*, the *bells I hear*, the *people all exulting*. (Whitman, 'O Captain! My Captain!')

   The poet presents a climactic development of events as a ship is welcomed by people at the harbour.

7. A *speck*, a *mist*, a *shape*, I wist!
   And still it neared and neared.
   (Coleridge, 'The Rime of the Ancient Mariner')

   The narrator sees a ghost ship nearing. Its size increases from 'a speck' to 'a shape'.

8. Their colours and their forms, were then to me
   An *appetite*; a *feeling* and a *love* (Wordsworth, 'Tintern Abbey')

   The poet talks about his feelings for nature.

9. A perfect woman, nobly planned,
   To *warm*, to *comfort*, and *command*.
   (Wordsworth, 'She Was a Phantom of Delight')

A woman's affectionate, supportive, and guiding qualities are referred to in an ascending order of seriousness.

10. That *consolation*, that *joy*, that *triumph*, was afforded him. (Southey, *The Life of Horatio, Lord Nelson*)

11. ... *black* it stood *as Night* / *Fierce as* ten *Furies*, terrible as Hell (Milton, *Paradise Lost*)

12. *Simple, erect, severe, austere, sublime* (Byron, *Childe Harold's Pilgrimage*)

13. We *grieved*, we *sighed*, we *wept* (Cowley, *Concerning the Government of Oliver Cromwell*)

14. All that most *maddens and torments*, all that *stirs up the lees of things*, all *truth with malice in it*, all that *cracks the sinews* and *cakes the brain*, all the *subtle demonisms of life and thought*, all *evil*, to crazy Ahab, were visibly personified and made practically assailable in Moby Dick. (Melville, *Moby Dick*)

ANTICLIMAX AND BATHOS

Anticlimax consists of a sudden decline from a serious or sublime idea to a trivial or ridiculous idea. Eighteenth-century literature contains many excellent examples of its effective use to create satire. Alexander Pope was a master of anticlimax, as can be seen in the following example from *The Rape of the Lock*:

> Here thou, great Anna! whom three realms obey,
> Dost sometimes counsel take—and sometimes tea.

The progression from 'counsel' to 'tea' is a sudden but *intended* fall from the lofty to the trivial, resulting in a comic satirical effect.

Anticlimax and **bathos** are often used as equivalent terms to signify a descent from lofty thought to the mundane and the trivial. Both create a comic effect. However, there is an important difference: bathos is unwittingly created by a less-than-capable poet and discovered by the informed reader. Trying to say something serious, the poet says something that comes across as silly. The resulting hilarious effect is *unintentional*. Lacking the necessary command over appropriate expression, the poet makes a fool of himself. Anticlimax, on the other hand, is *consciously applied* by the poet to create a comic effect. As Gordon Jarvie points out in the *Bloomsbury Grammar Guide*, bathos intends to be grave and impressive, but fails to hit the mark due to some inconsistency in the text.

The term (in its current sense) was introduced by Alexander Pope, who parodied Longinus's famous treatise *On the Sublime* in his essay *Peri Bathous, or the Art of Sinking in Poetry* (1727), in which he made fun of much of the poetry of his time. He offers to 'lead [the readers] as it were by the hand … the gentle downhill way to Bathos; the bottom, the end, the central point, the *non plus ultra*, of true Modern Poesy!'

Although Pope had mastered the art of using anticlimax, his poetry also fell to the depths of unintended bathos at least once, as seen in this example from *An Essay on Man*:

> The lamb thy riot dooms to bleed today,
> Had he thy reason, would he skip and play?
> Pleased to the last, he crops his flowery food,
> And licks the hand just raised to shed his blood.

Pope's complaint about the blindness of fate descends from a lofty question to juvenile sentimentality: trying to achieve the sublime, he slides down to the trivial image of a lamb licking its owner's hand. These lines are ridiculous: we laugh not *with* the poet, but *at* him.

Guided exercise

Given below are examples of anticlimax. Trace the fall of ideas from the lofty to the trivial.

1. *Sol* through white curtains *shot a timorous ray*,
   And *oped those eyes that must eclipse the day*;
   Now *lapdogs* give themselves the *rousing shake*,
   And *sleepless lovers*, just *at twelve, awake*.
   (Pope, *The Rape of the Lock*)

   Follow the series of ideas: the sun rises; Belinda's eyes, which are brighter than the sun, open; dogs shake themselves awake; and finally, lovers who boast of their lovesick 'sleeplessness' wake up at midday.

2. Not louder shrieks to pitying Heaven are cast,
   When *husbands*, or when *lapdogs*, breathe their last.
   (Pope, *The Rape of the Lock*)

3. A man so various that he seemed to be
   Not one, but all mankind's epitome:
   ... in the course of one revolving moon,
   Was *chemist, fiddler, statesman* and *buffoon*
   (Dryden, *Absalom and Achitophel*)

4. A better cavalier ne'er *mounted horse,*
   Or, being mounted, e'er *got down again* (Byron, *Don Juan*)

5. ... think how Bacon shined,
   The *wisest, brightest, meanest* of mankind!
   (Pope, *An Essay on Man*)

6. Sooner let earth, air, sea, to chaos fall,
   Men, monkeys, lapdogs, parrots, perish all!
   (Pope, *The Rape of the Lock*)

7. What *female heart* can *gold* despise?
   What *cat*'s averse to *fish*?
   (Gray, 'Ode on the Death of a Favourite Cat')

8. *Puffs, powders, patches, bibles, billet-doux*
   (Pope, *The Rape of the Lock*)

   This anticlimactic presentation of the items on Belinda's dressing table points to her confused system of values.

9. True Jedwood justice was dealt out to him. First came the *execution,* then the *investigation* and last of all ... the *accusation.*
   (Teresa Guiccioli, *My Recollections of Lord Byron*)

10. This piteous news, so *much it shocked her*
    She quite *forgot to send the doctor.*
    (Wordsworth, 'The Idiot Boy')

    There is an unintentional fall from the serious to the trivial, and hence these lines are an example of bathos.

SYLLEPSIS OR CONDENSED SENTENCE

Syllepsis (derived from the Greek for 'taking together') or the condensed sentence is a figure of speech in which a word is applied to two or more words in different senses, or a particular form of a word serves two or more words even though it agrees grammatically with only one of them. Let us examine this figure more closely with the help of examples.

In the first type of syllepsis, a word (usually a verb or a preposition) is used in a literal sense with relation to one noun, and in a figurative sense with relation to the other.

He <u>caught</u> a small fish and a cold this morning.

- The verb 'caught' connects two nouns, 'fish' and 'cold'.
- With relation to 'fish', the verb 'caught' literally means 'capturing'.
- With relation to 'cold', the verb 'caught' means 'contracted', that is, stricken with an illness. Here, we are playing with the figurative meaning of the word.
- Instead of resorting to a second verb such as 'contracted' or 'stricken' for the second noun, one verb is made to serve two nouns.

This trope thus allows a writer to convey an idea in a more compact manner (hence its other name, the 'condensed sentence'). However, the incongruous ways in which a single word is made to serve two ideas often make the resulting sentence sound funny or witty, or force us to pause and re-examine the line and its meaning. Syllepsis is therefore often found in **puns** (page 127) and in **epigrams** (page 48). It is a favourite device of comic writers because the absurd joining of odd, unmatched ideas excites laughter. For example:

The musician <u>blew</u> the pipe and his nose.

One verb ('blew') connects two nouns ('pipe' and 'nose'). The connected nouns/ideas are so different that placing them in parallel seems absurd and the result is hilarious. In *The Pickwick Papers*, Dickens writes:

... he <u>fell</u> into the barrow, and fast asleep ...

Many writers have found the condensed sentence to be a useful tool in their satirical works, as demonstrated by these lines from Pope's *The Rape of the Lock*:

Or <u>stain</u> her honour, or her new brocade, ...
Or <u>lose</u> her heart, or necklace, at a ball;

Syllepsis presents a contrast of the abstract and the concrete in a single line. One word ('stain') is used to cover two senses in the same expression. The first use of the verb is figurative ('stain her honour'), while the next use is literal ('stain her new brocade'). The effect is comic (two different ideas are absurdly linked), anticlimactic (there is a movement from a more important idea to a less important one), and satiric (Pope mocks a society that equates different values of unequal importance).

The second variety of syllepsis involves a deliberate flouting of grammatical agreement: one form of a verb is used to connect two nouns/pronouns/subjects, even though it agrees in number, tense or case with only one of them. The examples given below illustrate this very well.

Neither they nor it is working.

She and they have promised to come.

Look closely at the first example. The verb 'is working' connects the pronouns 'they' and 'it'. The phrase 'it is working' is grammatically correct; however, 'they is working' is not grammatically correct—it should be 'they are working'. Similarly, in the second example, the verb 'have promised' governs both 'she' and 'they', even though it grammatically suits only the latter—'she have promised' is incorrect.

Let us take an example of this type of condensed sentence from Shakespeare's *Othello*:

She has deceived her father, and may thee.

The same verb, 'has deceived', is used to connect two subjects, 'her father' and 'thee', despite the fact that such a construction is grammatically incorrect. The grammatically correct construction requires the use of separate forms of that verb: 'She *has deceived* her father, and may *deceive* thee'. In a well-constructed condensed sentence, the reader does not usually notice the grammatical incongruity at first glance.

See also **zeugma**, page 114.

Guided exercise

Explain the figure of speech in the lines below. The connected ideas have been italicised for you, while the connecting verbs or prepositions have been underlined.

1. I had fancied you were gone down to underline{cultivate} *matrimony* and your *estate in the country*. (Goldsmith, *Citizen of the World*)

2. ... where the *washing* is not put out, nor the *fire*, nor the *mistress* ... (Thoreau, *Walden*)

3. Among the tyrants who rebelled against the king, there was none who <u>enjoyed</u> *a life of peace* or *a natural death.*

4. <u>Obliged</u> by *hunger* and *request of friends*
(Pope, *Epistle to Dr Arbuthnot*)

5. Milton, having now tasted the honey of public employment, would not <u>return</u> to *hunger* and *philosophy*
(Johnson, *Lives of the Poets*)

6. Miss Bolo ... went straight home, <u>in</u> a *flood of tears* and a *sedan chair.* (Dickens, *The Pickwick Papers*)

7. He <u>works</u> *his* work, I *mine.* (Tennyson, 'Ulysses')

8. Either *they* or I <u>am wrong.</u>

9. ... <u>rend</u> your *heart* and not your *garments* ...
(The Book of Joel)

10. Mr Stiggins ... <u>took</u> *his hat* and *his leave*
(Dickens, *The Pickwick Papers*)

PARADOX

Paradox is a self-contradicting statement that may sound absurd but lays emphasis on a valid central idea. Whether the paradox can be separated from the epigram is a debatable issue. While some commentators say that the paradox is a *quality* shared by the epigram and the oxymoron, others recognise it as a distinct tool used by G.K. Chesterton and Oscar Wilde for social criticism. In either case, paradox is characterised by its ability to transvaluate normative social truth. It has a subversive power that compels the reader to rethink accepted truths.

Wilde's epigrams are slightly different from standard epigrams in this respect. Consider the following epigrams side by side:

> Our antagonist is our helper. (Burke)
> Consistency is the last refuge of the unimaginative. (Wilde)

We clearly see that while both examples are brief and witty, there is a difference in the degree of the shock they create. The second example is much more subversive: it wages war against the contemporary Victorian culture of seriousness. Consistency, coherence, seriousness and uniformity were highly valued qualities back then, and Wilde is dethroning them through transvaluation, the hallmark of paradox. However, Wilde's quotes are widely recognised as epigrams, and students are advised to point them out as such, recognising paradox as a *quality* found in both epigrams and oxymorons.

> Season of mists and mellow fruitfulness,
> Close bosom-friend of the maturing sun;
> Conspiring with him how to load and bless
> With fruit the vines that round the thatch-eves run ...
> ... to set budding more,
> And still more, later flowers for the bees,
> Until they think warm days will never cease,
> For summer has o'er-brimm'd their clammy cells.

The 'season of mists and mellow fruitfulness'—autumn—is personified here. Autumn conspires with her close friend, the sun (another personification), to bring about fruitfulness in nature ('load and bless'). Mark the human attribute of friendship between autumn and the sun. Summer and the bees are other personified participants in this mysterious process of seasonal change. In another beautiful image from this poem, the clouds are personified as an artist who paints a landscape in water colour:

> While barrèd clouds bloom the soft-dying day,
> And touch the stubble-plains with rosy hue

The two action verbs employed to create this personification are 'bloom' (a water colour technique of adding soft warm hues) and 'touch' (painting with light brush-strokes).

Personification and the transferred epithet

Look at these lines from Owen's 'Dulce et Decorum Est', which describe soldiers marching to the front when they are suddenly shelled with poison gas:

> Drunk with fatigue; deaf even to the hoots
> Of gas-shells dropping softly behind.
> Gas! Gas! Quick, boys!—An ecstasy of fumbling
> Fitting the clumsy helmets just in time ...

The phrase 'hoots / Of gas-shells' is a personification. The gas-shells are imagined as hooting (letting out shrill, derisive cries), like a person might.

The phrase 'clumsy helmets', on the other hand, is *not* a personification, but another figure with which it is occasionally confused: the **transferred epithet** (page 41). This rhetorical device involves shifting an adjective (that is usually reserved for a person) to an inanimate object, as in the phrases 'cheerful money' or 'sleepless night'. The human attributes of cheerfulness, sleeplessness or (as in the example from Owen above) clumsiness are deliberately misapplied to inanimate entities such as 'money', 'night' and 'helmets'. This is why some students confuse it with personification. However, there is a clear difference between the two.

The key to distinguishing between a transferred epithet and personification is to ask the question: *Who* is the *subject* of the line? To whom does the epithet actually apply?

- The transferred epithet deliberately applies an adjective (human quality) to an inanimate noun, instead of applying it to the human subject.
- In a personification, the personified entity is the subject, and the adjective (human quality) relates to the subject itself.

The examples that follow will help clarify this.

The ploughman homeward plods his weary way. (Gray, 'Elegy')

- Who is the *subject*? Who is 'weary'?
- Answer: 'The ploughman' (not 'way')
- The epithet (adjective) is transferred from the subject ('ploughman', a human) to something else ('way', an inanimate thing).
- Therefore, 'weary way' is a transferred epithet.

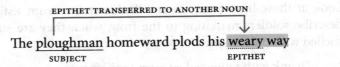

EPITHET TRANSFERRED TO ANOTHER NOUN

The <u>ploughman</u> homeward plods his weary way
SUBJECT   EPITHET

The thirsty earth soaks up the rain (Cowley, 'Drinking')

- Who is the *subject*? Who is 'thirsty'?
- Answer: The earth
- The epithet (adjective) applies to the inanimate subject itself.
- Therefore, 'thirsty earth' is a personification.

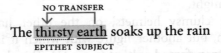

NO TRANSFER

The thirsty earth soaks up the rain
EPITHET SUBJECT

Three sleepless nights I passed ... (Wordsworth, *The Borderers*)

- Who is the *subject*? Who is 'sleepless'?
- Answer: 'I' (not 'nights')
- The epithet (adjective) is transferred from the subject ('I', a human) to something else ('nights', an inanimate thing).
- Therefore, 'sleepless nights' is a transferred epithet.

I have seen the hungry ocean gain / Advantage ...
(Shakespeare, 'Sonnet 64')

- Who is the *subject*? Who is 'hungry'?
- Answer: The ocean
- The epithet (adjective) applies to the inanimate subject itself.
- Therefore, 'hungry ocean' is a personification.

When trying to distinguish between personification and transferred epithet, check *who* is thinking/feeling/performing an action. If this is being done by a non-human agent, it is personification. If there is a human agent—who need not always be explicitly mentioned, and may be merely implied—it is an instance of transferred epithet.

Guided exercise

Explain the figure of speech in the lines given below. The non-human entities are underlined.

1. Nor *heaven peep through* the blanket of the dark
   To cry 'Hold! Hold!' (Shakespeare, *Macbeth*)

2. But *patience, to prevent* / That murmur, soon *replies*
   (Milton, 'On His Blindness')

3. *Fear* at my heart, as at a cup,
   My life-blood seemed to *sip*!
   (Coleridge, 'The Rime of the Ancient Mariner')

4. And now the *storm-blast came*, and *he*
   Was tyrannous and strong
   (Coleridge, 'The Rime of the Ancient Mariner')

5. How sweet the *moonlight sleeps* upon this bank!
   (Shakespeare, *The Merchant of Venice*)

6. Let *nature* be your *teacher*. (Wordsworth, 'The Tables Turned')

7. *Fair tresses* man's imperial race *ensnare*
   (Pope, *The Rape of the Lock*)

8. Chill *Penury repressed* their noble rage,
   And *froze* the genial current of the soul.
   (Gray, 'Elegy Written in a Country Churchyard')

   Note the transferred epithet 'noble rage' in the above lines.

9. But *Knowledge* to their eyes *her* ample page
   Rich with the spoils of time *did ne'er unroll*
   (Gray, 'Elegy Written in a Country Churchyard')

10. Thine *azure sister of the Spring shall blow*
    Her clarion o'er the *dreaming earth*
    (Shelley, 'Ode to the West Wind)

    There are two personifications here. The east wind of spring
    (the 'sister' of the autumnal west wind) is represented as
    blowing her trumpet to awaken the earth, which is asleep and
    dreaming.

11. *Death closes* all (Tennyson, 'Ulysses')

12. *Philosophy will clip* an angel's wings. (Keats, *Lamia*)

13. *Love*'s not *Time*'s *fool*. (Shakespeare, 'Sonnet 116')

14. But at my back I always hear
    Time's winged chariot *hurrying* near.
    (Marvell, 'To His Coy Mistress')

15. The flowers the *wanton Zephyrs choose*
    (Wordsworth, 'To the Daisy')

16. *Death lays his* icy *hand* on kings
    (Shirley, 'The Glories of Our Blood and State')

    Mark the use of the verb 'lays', the personal pronoun 'his', and
    the noun 'hand' that properly belongs to a human being.

17. The *train panted* at last into Paddington station
    (Chesterton, 'The Secret of a Train')

    The train is imagined to be exhausted.

18. And their *great pines groan aghast* (Shelley, 'The Cloud')

    The pine trees are imagined to be crying in pain.

We will now look at three varieties of personification in a little
more detail. These are **prosopopoeia**, **personal metaphor**, and
pathetic fallacy.

PROSOPOPOEIA

Prosopopoeia is a special kind of personification where a dead or absent person, or a personified entity, is represented as speaking. St Paul, in '1 Corinthians' (a book in the Bible), argues:

> If the foot shall say, 'Because I am not the hand, I am not of the body'; Is it therefore not of the body? And if the ear shall say, 'Because I am not the eye, I am not of the body'; is it therefore not of the body?

Here, the foot and the ear are imagined as speaking.

Prosopopoeia is a kind of impersonation. In the *Institutio Oratoria*, Quintilian comments that prosopopoeia is:

> a device which lends wonderful variety and animation to oratory. By this means we display the inner thoughts of our adversaries as though they were talking with themselves ... we are even allowed in this form of speech to bring down the gods from heaven and raise the dead, while cities also and peoples may find a voice.

Beginner-orators in ancient Greece and Rome were given exercises in which they had to impersonate others and speak from their points of view. This was done in order to provide a certain perspective, to counter an argument, or to distance the orator from an unpopular opinion. Former President of the United States Barack Obama used this technique in a speech advocating gun control, where he imagines the responses that his speech would provoke among the gun lobby:

> Right now, I can imagine the press releases being cranked out: 'We need more guns', they'll argue. 'Fewer gun safety laws.'

He does this in order to pre-emptively counter these arguments and make his case stronger.

As Gavin Alexander observes, prosopopoeia enables a speaker to wear a mask and speak in the voices of others ('Prosopopeia: The Speaking Figure'). Mute objects or silent subjects can be given a human face and a voice. An obvious example is Shelley's lyric 'The Cloud': the entire poem uses this device.

> I am the daughter of Earth and Water,
> And the nursling of the Sky;

I pass through the pores of the ocean and shores;
I change, but I cannot die.

The literary critic and theorist Paul de Man considered prosopopoeia the 'master trope' of poetic expression (*Resistance to Theory*) because all writing or speech is representation.

PERSONAL METAPHOR

Personal metaphor is the name given to a specific type of personification in which an element of nature is endowed with personality through the use of adjectives (or participial adjectives or adjective phrases). Expressions such as 'frowning sky', 'prattling brook', 'sullen sea', and 'threatening storm' are personal metaphors. This device describes an inanimate object as if it were a living person.

This form of personification is referred to as a 'metaphor' because it involves an implicit comparison between a person and nature. Like all metaphors, the above examples can be expanded into similes: 'the sky is frowning like an irritated person' or 'the brook prattles like a little child'. The tenor (the subject of the comparison, 'sky', 'brook') is mentioned along with the point of comparison ('frowning', 'prattling'), which is always an adjective that should properly be ascribed to a person. The vehicle (the object of the comparison, 'irritated person', 'little child') is not explicitly mentioned, and is always a human. See **Constructing a metaphor**, page 24.

The personal metaphor is an attractive device in writing because the vocabulary expressing the various moods of a person is richer than that describing natural objects. Use of the personal metaphor can be seen in the following line from Cowley's poem 'Drinking':

The thirsty earth soaks up the rain

Look at the adjective 'thirsty' in the above example: the earth is supplied with an attribute appropriate to a person. This personification metaphorically compares the earth (an inanimate thing) to a thirsty person. Here is another example, from Elinor Wylie's 'The Eagle and the Mole':

Live like that stoic bird,
The eagle of the rock.

Shakespeare uses this trope in 'Sonnet 64' when he says:

> When I have seen the hungry ocean gain
> Advantage on the kingdom of the shore

Please note carefully that these are *not* examples of transferred epithets. The epithets 'thirsty', 'stoic' and 'hungry' apply directly to the inanimate subjects 'earth', 'bird' and 'ocean'; they have not been transferred from a different noun or a hidden subject. See **Personification and the transferred epithet**, page 67.

Finally, it must be stated here that *all* forms of personifications are, broadly speaking, **metaphors** (page 23) because all personification figuratively and implicitly likens one noun (a natural or inanimate object, or an abstract idea) to another (specifically, a person). The personal metaphor is a particular species of personification in which the subject is an element of nature, and in which the comparison is made through an adjective that properly applies to a human being.

PATHETIC FALLACY

Pathetic fallacy is personification taken to its logical extreme in which an inanimate object (usually nature or a natural object) is shown to be actively sympathetic or hostile towards human beings. In pathetic fallacy, the natural world feels, understands and reflects the moods and emotions of the poetic persona or of a character in a literary text. See, for example, the following line from Wordsworth's 'Yarrow Visited':

> Bear witness rueful Yarrow!

The Yarrow river is not only asked to give testimony, but also attributed with the human emotion 'rueful' because it *shares* the sense of sadness and regret that the poet experiences.

The term 'pathetic fallacy' was coined by the influential Victorian critic John Ruskin, who used it to mean 'false emotion'—inanimate objects do not have emotions ('pathos'), he emphasised, and so the attribution of feelings and motives to them is a kind of falseness ('fallacy') or error. In *Modern Painters* (Volume III, 1856), he opined that emotional 'distortion' had characterised art and literature since the Romantic period, which had placed great value on 'excited state[s] of the feelings'. Measured by Victorian standards of propriety, these excesses seemed irrational and inappropriate: 'All violent feelings … produce in us a falseness in all our impressions of external things'. Ruskin draws our attention to the following lines from Charles Kingsley's poem 'The Sands o' Dee' as overly emotional:

> They rowed her in across the rolling foam,—
> The cruel, crawling foam

Grief has so distorted the mind of the poet, Ruskin argues, that he has attributed to the foam the sinister intentions of a person. Let us take another example, from 'The Comforters' by Dora Sigerson Shorter:

> When I stood lone by thy cross, sorrow did speak.
> When I went down the long hill, I cried and I cried.
> The soft little hands of the rain stroked my pale cheek,
> The kind little feet of the rain ran by my side.

The rain is imagined as a small child consoling the bereaved speaker. Ruskin used the term 'pathetic fallacy' to attack such sentimental ascriptions of sympathetic behaviour to indifferent nature. However, in modern usage the term has lost any derogatory connotation that Ruskin intended and is used in a neutral sense to refer to this particular variety of personification.

In the hands of skilful writers, pathetic fallacy can become a great tool for myth-making. In the following passage from Shakespeare's *Hamlet*, Horatio describes the effect of the death of a great ruler:

> In the most high and palmy state of Rome,
> A little ere the mightiest Julius fell,
> The graves stood tenantless and the sheeted dead
> Did squeak and gibber in the Roman streets
> As stars with trains of fire and dews of blood,
> Disasters in the sun, and the moist star
> Upon whose influence Neptune's empire stands
> Was sick almost to doomsday with eclipse.

In *Macbeth*, the night of Duncan's murder is described thus:

> The night has been unruly: where we lay,
> Our chimneys were blown down; and, as they say,
> Lamentings heard i' the air; …
> … some say, the earth
> Was feverous and did shake.

Nature is shocked by the crime. Similarly, the storms in *King Lear* and *Wuthering Heights* reflect the inner turmoil of the characters in these works. In the following passage from Pope's *Pastorals*, a series of pathetic fallacies are used to describe all nature mourning the death of Daphne:

> Fair Daphne's dead, and music is no more!
> Her fate is whisper'd by the gentle breeze,
> And told in sighs to all the trembling trees;
> The trembling trees, in every plain and wood,
> Her fate remurmur to the silver flood;
> The silver flood, so lately calm, appears
> Swell'd with new passion, and o'erflows with tears;
> The winds and trees and floods her death deplore,
> Daphne, our Grief, our Glory now no more!

Not only are the winds, trees and streams personified, but they are seen acting in sympathy with the poetic persona who mourns a loss. Pathetic fallacy thus involves extreme anthropomorphism. Take a look at the following lines from Henry Derozio's 'A Walk by Moonlight':

> The moon stood silent in the sky,
> And looked upon our earth:
> The clouds divided, passing by,
> In homage to her worth.
>
> There was a dance among the leaves
> Rejoicing at her power,
> Who robes for them of silver weaves
> Within one mystic hour.

The magical moonlight arouses a deep sense of reverence in the poet. Clouds and leaves are depicted as sharing this feeling of reverence. In the poem 'Anthem for Doomed Youth', Wilfred Owen personifies the bombs ('shells') raining down upon soldiers:

> Nor any voice of mourning save the choirs,—
> The shrill, demented choirs of wailing shells

Owen's sorrow at the senseless waste of war is reflected in the shrill weeping of the shells.

Guided exercise

Explain the figure of speech in the lines given below. Hints are provided.

1. *Nature might stand up / And say to all the world, 'This was a man.'* (Shakespeare, *Julius Caesar*)

   Nature is imagined to be proud of a person. Note that there is also prosopopoeia in this line.

2. Earth felt the wound, and *Nature* from her seat
   Sighing through all her works, *gave signs of woe*
   (Milton, *Paradise Lost*)

   Nature is left stunned by mankind's disobedience of God's will.

3. When from her lips her soul took wing;
   The *oaks forgot their pondering*,
   The *pines their reverie*. (William Watson, 'Song')

   Oaks and pines stop musing and dreaming when the poet's lover dies.

4. The *heavens themselves blaze forth the death of princes*.
   (Shakespeare, *Julius Caesar*)

A note on the varieties of personification

Prosopopoeia, personal metaphor and pathetic fallacy are three modes of personification. All three of them represent an abstract quality or idea or a non-human thing as a person.

- In prosopopoeia, the personified entity is imagined as speaking like a human being.
  The land cried out: 'We are suffering; give us justice!'

- In personal metaphor, an aspect of nature is personified by employing adjectives reserved for human beings.
  The suffering land could no longer bear the injustice.

- In pathetic fallacy, an aspect of nature thinks, feels and/or acts in a way that expresses either harmony with or hostility towards human beings.
  The land wept at the suffering of its people.

It should be kept in mind that there might, occasionally, be some overlap between some of these terms. In such cases, the context might help one differentiate between them:

The stubborn boulder braved the onslaught of the waves.

PERSONAL METAPHOR

A stubborn boulder barred her way.   PATHETIC FALLACY

APOSTROPHE

The word 'apostrophe' derives from a Greek word that means turning away from the present audience to address someone else. It is a figure of speech where a writer or a speaker turns away from the main subject and makes a sudden, short and impassioned address to an absent or dead person, or an imaginary person or entity, or something non-human, or a place, or an abstract idea. Needless to say, this is an interruption of an ongoing discourse.

Take a look at an example from Shakespeare's *Julius Caesar*:

O judgement! Thou art fled to brutish beasts

'Judgement' is apostrophised here, that is, the abstract idea of impartial decision has been directly and powerfully addressed by the speaker (and not merely imagined to be a person, as we see in **personification**). The apostrophe is also called 'passive personification', as abstract ideas or inanimate objects passively listen to the address of the speaker or writer.

The apostrophe is an essential element in the ode, the most elevated form of lyric poetry. Jonathan Culler comments on the role of this rhetorical trope: 'they serve as intensifiers, as images of invested passion'; the apostrophising poet turns his back to the audience and communicates with the living forces of the universe. If Blake had said 'the rose is sick', his verse would lack passion and immediacy. By apostrophising and saying 'O Rose, thou art sick', he communicates with the pulsating universe around him while the audience overhears his conversation.

Guided exercise

Explain the figure of speech in the lines given below. Key words are italicised, and hints are provided.

Address to a **dead person**

1. *Milton!* Thou shouldst be living in this hour:
   England hath need of thee (Wordsworth, 'London, 1802')

2. *My mother!* When I learnt thou wast dead,
   Say, wast thou conscious of the tears I shed?
   (Cowper, 'On the Receipt of My Mother's Picture')

Address to a **living but absent person**

3. *O, Friend!* I know not which way I must look / For comfort ...
   (Wordsworth, 'Written in London. September, 1802')

4. *Men of England*, wherefore plough
   For the lords who lay ye low?
   (Shelley, 'Song to the Men of England')
   The poet addresses his countrymen who are absent at the spot.

Address to a **deity** (see also **invocation**, page 79)

5. *Mary Mother*, save me now!
   (Said Christabel) And who art thou? (Coleridge, 'Christabel')

Address to an **imaginary person or thing**

6. Out, *damned spot!* Out, I say! (Shakespeare, *Macbeth*)

Address to an **abstract idea**

7. *O, Solitude!* where are the charms
   That sages have seen in thy face?
   (Cowper, 'The Solitude of Alexander Selkirk')

8. *O death*, where is thy sting? *O grave*, where is thy victory?
   (St Paul, '1 Corinthians')

9. *O luxury!* thou curst by Heaven's decree,
   How ill exchanged are things like these for thee!
   (Goldsmith, *The Deserted Village*)

Address to a **country, nation, or city**

10. *England*, with all thy faults, I love thee still (Cowper, *The Task*)

11. *Italia! oh Italia!* thou who hast
    The fatal gift of beauty (Byron, *Childe Harold's Pilgrimage*)

12. Wave, *Munich!* All thy banners wave,
    And charge with all thy chivalry! (Campbell, 'Hohenlinden')

Address to the **natural world** (phenomena, geographical features, flora, fauna)

13. *Hail, holy Light!* offspring of Heaven first-born!
    (Milton, *Paradise Lost*)
    The poet addresses a natural phenomenon.

14. ... Come, *thick night*
    And pall thee in the dunnest smoke of Hell
    (Shakespeare, *Macbeth*)
    The speaker addresses a natural phenomenon.

15. *O wild West Wind*, thou breath of Autumn's being
    (Shelley, 'Ode to the West Wind')
    The poet addresses a natural force.

16. *O Greta*, dear domestic stream!
    (Coleridge, 'Recollections of Love')
    The poet addresses a river.

17. *O sylvan Wye!* Thou wanderer through the wood,
    How often has my spirit turned to thee!
    (Wordsworth, 'Tintern Abbey')
    The poet addresses a river.

18. *Hail* to thee, *blithe spirit!* (Shelley, 'To a Skylark')
    The poet addresses a bird.

Address to an **inanimate object**

19. *Thou* still unravished *bride of quietness*
    (Keats, 'Ode on a Grecian Urn')
    The poet addresses a vase used for preserving the ashes of the dead.

INVOCATION

Invocation is a direct and impassioned prayer for creative inspiration, made by a poet to a supernatural being, usually the Muses—classical goddesses, among whom were Calliope (representing epic poetry), Urania (astronomy and highest knowledge) and Clio (fame and history).

Traditionally, epic poetry got its subject from history, which meant that readers already knew the story. The poet is empowered as he becomes part of a tradition, but at the same time he is handicapped by it. Invocation subtly shifts the focus from tradition to *inspiration*—the poet is possessed by a mysterious creative power and can now re-tell the story in a significantly different way. The following passages are from the opening stanza of Milton's *Paradise Lost*:

> Sing Heav'nly Muse, that on the secret top
> Of Oreb, or of Sinai, didst inspire
> That Shepherd, who first taught the chosen Seed ...
>
> And chiefly Thou O Spirit, that dost prefer
> Before all Temples th' upright heart and pure,
> Instruct me ...

One needs to note that these extracts are not merely impassioned addresses to a deity (see **apostrophe**, page 77) but also prayers for creative inspiration which would enable the poet to accomplish his enormous task. This unique feature of the address makes them instances of invocation.

VISION

This figure consists in the description of an absent or imaginary object or image in so picturesque a way that it appears to be present before the senses. The writer or speaker uses the present tense (instead of the past or future) and it seems the event is present before her or his eyes.

In Shakespeare's *Macbeth*, for example, before killing Duncan, Macbeth can see the vision of a sword:

> Is this a dagger which I see before me,
> The handle toward my hand? Come, let me clutch thee.
> I have thee not, and yet I see thee still.
> Art thou not, fatal vision, sensible
> To feeling as to sight? or art thou but
> A dagger of the mind, a false creation,
> Proceeding from the heat-oppressed brain?
> I see thee yet, in form as palpable
> As this which now I draw.
> Thou marshall'st me the way that I was going;
> And such an instrument I was to use.

Mine eyes are made the fools o' the other senses,
Or else worth all the rest; I see thee still,
And on thy blade and dudgeon gouts of blood,
Which was not so before.

In Sir Walter Raleigh's short poem 'A Vision upon the Fairy Queen'
we find some apt examples of the use of vision:

Methought I saw the grave where Laura lay,
Within that temple where the vestal flame
Was wont to burn; and, passing by that way,
To see that buried dust of living fame,
Whose tomb fair Love, and fairer Virtue kept:
All suddenly I saw the Fairy Queen;
At whose approach the soul of Petrarch wept,
And, from thenceforth, those Graces were not seen:
For they this queen attended; in whose stead
Oblivion laid him down on Laura's hearse:
Hereat the hardest stones were seen to bleed,
And groans of buried ghosts the heavens did pierce:
Where Homer's spright did tremble all for grief,
And cursed the access of that celestial thief!

Exercise

Explain the figure of speech in the lines given below.

1. Pride in their port, defiance in their eye,
   I see the lords of human kind pass by (Goldsmith, *The Traveller*)

2. Hark! forth from the abyss a voice proceeds,
   A long low distant murmur of dread sound.
   (Byron, *Childe Harold's Pilgrimage*)

3. Methinks I see in my mind a noble and puissant nation rousing
   herself like a strong man after sleep, and shaking her invincible
   locks; methinks I see her as an eagle mewing her mighty youth,
   and kindling her undazzled eyes at the full midday beam.
   (Milton, *Areopagitica*)

4. I see the hands a nation's lyre that strung,
   The eyes that looked through life and gazed on God.
   (William Watson, 'Lachrymæ Musarum')

5. Even now, methinks, as pondering here I stand,
    I see the rural virtues leave the land
    (Goldsmith, *The Deserted Village*)

HYPERBOLE

Hyperbole is a deliberate and extravagant exaggeration. It consists in expressing a thing as greater or less, better or worse, than it really is, in order to produce a strong impression in the mind. A hyperbole can be expressed by a number, a word, a clause, a sentence, or lexical choice in a passage.

In the following example from Shakespeare's *Hamlet*, the protagonist uses a hyperbole to express his love for the dead Ophelia:

> I loved Ophelia. Forty thousand brothers
> Could not, with all their quantity of love,
> Make up my sum.

A hyperbolical statement is not meant to be literal: Claudia Claridge observes that the former characteristically exceeds the limits of credibility in a particular context. 'Forty thousand brothers' is an absurd figure: obviously, both the speaker and his audience know that it is an overstatement, not a lie or mistake. The expression is a departure from literal truth in order to express a deeper, emotional truth: a brother's affection for his sister was incomparable to Hamlet's profound love for Ophelia.

As an intensifier, hyperbole can be used to give an impression of plentitude, immensity and vastness. Quintilian in *Institutio* recognises hyperbole as an elegant surpassing of truth:

> Hyperbole lies, but not so as to intend to deceive by lying. ... It is in common use, as much among the unlearned as among the learned; because there is in all men a natural propensity to magnify or extenuate what comes before them, and no one is contented with the exact truth. But such departure from the truth is pardoned, because we do not affirm what is false. In a word, the hyperbole is a beauty, when the thing itself, of which we have to speak, is in its nature extraordinary; for we are then allowed to say a little more than the truth, because the exact truth cannot be said; and language is more efficient when it goes beyond reality than when it stops short of it.

Let us take an example from 'Daffodils', where Wordsworth claims:

> Ten thousand saw I at a glance.

The poet came across a great number of daffodils while on a walk. This overwhelming presence is expressed through the hyperbolic statement that he saw 'ten thousand' at a glance. The numerical hyperbole works as an intensifier.

Hyperbole can be used not only for the purpose of emotional intensification but also satirical sabotaging. Andrew Marvell's lyric 'To His Coy Mistress' uses a series of famous hyperboles to mock the tradition of courtly love poetry. The poetic persona tells his mistress that 'Had [they] but world enough, and time', he would spend all eternity courting her. This hypothetical scenario is imagined using a rapid succession of hyperboles. To begin with, the lover posits impossible stretches of space where they might play long-distance games of courtship: the lady would spend time along the banks of the River Ganges in India, while the lover woo her from that of the River Humber in England:

> Thou by the Indian Ganges' side
> Shouldst rubies find; I by the tide
> Of Humber would complain.

In the lines that follow, hyperbolical clauses propose absurd Biblical time-frames for his proposal and her eventual acceptance of his love:

> I would
> Love you ten years before the flood,
> And you should, if you please, refuse
> Till the conversion of the Jews.

The poetic hyperbole continues as the speaker talks about their love spreading over a vast area over millennia, and about how he would spend years praising her beauty.

> My vegetable love should grow
> Vaster than empires and more slow;
> An hundred years should go to praise
> Thine eyes, and on thy forehead gaze;
> Two hundred to adore each breast,
> But thirty thousand to the rest;
> An age at least to every part ...

However, the speaker presents these hyperboles in order to deflate the idea behind them. The lovers do not, in fact, have all the time in the world: time moves quickly (an idea made memorable by the famous metaphor of a winged chariot); this imagined scheme is impractical; the lovers must make haste. These hyperboles comically expose the gap between expectation and reality. They effectively assail the lady's demureness and indecision, and prompt her to enjoy youth while it lasts. In Marvell's poem, hyperbole is a weapon used for witty sabotage.

Jonathan Swift's satirical essay 'A Modest Proposal' was a sardonic attack on the English exploitation of Ireland. It advocated a unique solution for Ireland's poverty: the Irish could sell their children as food for the English!

> I have been assured ... that a young healthy child, well nursed, is, at a year old, a most delicious, nourishing, and wholesome food; whether stewed, roasted, baked, or boiled; and I make no doubt, that it will equally serve in a fricassée or ragout.

Cooking and eating children as a solution to Ireland's poverty is, of course, a hyperbole designed to shock the reader: it is not meant be taken literally. Swift's intention was to scandalise and attack the insensitive English reader, and make him recognise that England's treatment of the Irish people was no better than cannibalism.

The era of Swift, Dryden and Pope was an age of satire. Hyperbole, along with **allusion** (page 42) and **irony** (page 92), was a major tool in the service of satire, through which inflated images of authoritative personages were punctured and contemporary social mores ridiculed. To achieve this, the poet would often allude to grand, heroic or mythical events while describing trivial contemporary reality. Such hyperbole would connect these incompatible events in an absurd expression that would accentuate the pettiness of the celebrated present.

In Pope's *The Rape of the Lock*, the poet's presentation of the protagonist Belinda is hyperbolical. She is presented as a 'goddess' whose eyes 'eclipse the day'. Her dressing for the tea-party is likened to the arming of an epic hero for battle: 'Now awful beauty puts on all its arms'. This exaggeration is a deliberate allusion to classical epics such as the *Iliad* and the *Aeneid*. However, just like Marvell in 'Coy Mistress', Pope uses hyperbole to ironically undercut the pomposity of his peers. The exaggeration and the allusions forcefully remind us that the age of heroes is long gone.

Hyperbole and metaphor

A **metaphor** (page 23) is a figure of speech that compares two entities which are similar based on a specific point of comparison. A hyperbole always exaggerates and exceeds the credible limits of a comparison. For example, in *The Rape of the Lock*, Pope talks about Belinda's 'eyes that … eclipse the day'. The heroine's eyes are so bright that they *outshine* the sun. There is indeed a comparison (Belinda's eyes are compared to the sun), but instead of similarity ('as bright as') we have an exaggeration which crosses the limit of credibility (a person cannot have eyes brighter than the sun). The reader must look past the literal meaning of the line in order to arrive at the deeper meaning intended by the hyperbole—Belinda has bright, lively eyes.

Hyperbole through lexical choice

Two of the most important hyperboles in *The Rape of the Lock* are not one-liners, but extended comparisons that equate an ordinary event to something epic. Through the lexical choices made by the poet in each passage, the first extract below likens dressing to a religious ritual, and the second one equates the cutting of Belinda's hair with war (and war-crimes). These comparisons are non-metaphorical. Instead of a point of comparison, there is a huge gap between the epic world depicted by the lexical choice and the true nature of Pope's contemporary cultural reality. The incongruity created by the hyperbolical comparison leads to satire.

The first passage is the description of Belinda's toilet in Canto I.

> And now, unveiled, the toilet stands displayed,
> Each silver vase in mystic order laid.
> First, robed in white, the nymph intent adores,
> With head uncovered, the cosmetic powers.
> A heavenly image in the glass appears,
> To that she bends, to that her eyes she rears;
> The inferior priestess, at her altar's side,
> Trembling begins the sacred rites of pride.
> Unnumbered treasures ope at once, and here
> The various offerings of the world appear;
> For each she nicely culls with curious toil,

> And decks the goddess with the glittering spoil.
> This casket India's glowing gems unlocks,
> And all Arabia breathes from yonder box.

There are two hyperboles at work here. Through a careful choice words (highlighted for you), Belinda's toilet is raised to the absurd level of a religious ceremony. This hyperbole exaggerates the contemporary importance given to women's beautification, thus belittling and satirising the hollowness of her culture. A second hyperbole is at work in the last few lines (see the underlined words). This hyperbole comments on the increasingly global commerce that brought various consumer products from all over the world to Belinda's dressing table to be used to create a shallow, unproductive culture of beauty.

The next passage is from Canto III, the incident of the 'rape', that is, the clipping of Belinda's lock:

> Just then, Clarissa drew with tempting grace
> A two-edged weapon from her shining case;
> So ladies in romance assist their knight,
> Present the spear, and arm him for the fight.
> He takes the gift with reverence, and extends
> The little engine on his finger's ends;
> This just behind Bellinda's neck he spread, ...
> Thrice she looked back, and thrice the foe drew near. ...
> The peer now spreads the glittering forfex wide,
> To enclose the lock; now joins it, to divide.
> Even then, before the fatal engine closed,
> A wretched Sylph too fondly interposed;
> Fate urged the shears, and cut the Sylph in twain ...
> The meeting points the sacred hair dissever
> From the fair head, for ever and for ever! ...
> 'Let wreaths of triumph now my temples twine,'
> (The victor cried) 'the glorious prize is mine!'

The choice of words (highlighted) in the passage compares the trivial incident of the clipping of a lock of hair with an epic battle in the world of romance. A pair of scissors becomes 'the fatal engine' and the baron who shears the lock becomes the proud 'victor'. This hyperbole accentuates the triviality of Pope's contemporary city-bred upper-class society.

Guided exercise

Explain the figure of speech in the lines given below. Key words are italicised, and hints are provided.

1. Here's the smell of the blood still: *all the perfumes of Arabia will not sweeten this little hand.* Oh, oh, oh! (Shakespeare, *Macbeth*)

   The smell of blood is so overwhelming, and the sense of guilt so strong, that the speaker needs a hyperbolical statement to express herself.

2. But, soft! What light through yonder window breaks?
   It is the east, and Juliet is the sun.
   (Shakespeare, *Romeo and Juliet*)

3. To follow knowledge like a sinking star,
   Beyond the utmost bound of human thought.
   (Tennyson, 'Ulysses')

4. *Drink to me only with thine eyes,*
   And I will pledge with mine;
   Or *leave a kiss but in the cup,*
   And I'll not look for wine. (Jonson, 'Song: To Celia')

5. But *to see her was to love her,*
   Love but her, and love *for ever* (Burns, 'Ae Fond Kiss')
   Hyperbolic description of the speaker's ladylove

6. *The triumphal arch through which I march*
   With hurricane, fire, and snow,
   When the Powers of the air are chained to my chair,
   Is the million-coloured bow (Shelley, 'The Cloud')
   Hyperbolic description of the rainbow, the victory-arch of the cloud

7. It was *roses, roses, all the way,*
   With myrtle mixed in my path like mad;
   The house-roofs seemed to heave and sway,
   The church-spires flamed, such flags they had,
   A year ago on this very day. (Browning, 'The Patriot')

   The descriptions of the path on which the patriots walk, and the effects of the march on rooftops and church-spires, are exaggerated to convey the emotional impact of their movement.

8. O Hamlet! Thou hast *cleft my heart in twain*! (Shakespeare, *Hamlet*)

9. *To see a World in a Grain of Sand*
   And a Heaven in a Wild Flower
   Hold Infinity in the palm of your hand
   And Eternity in an hour (Blake, 'Auguries of Innocence')

10. Saul and Jonathan were lovely and pleasant in their lives, and in their death they were not divided: *they were swifter than eagles, they were stronger than lions*. (The Book of Samuel)

See also **litotes**, page 102.

FIVE

Figures based on Indirectness

INNUENDO

Innuendo is an indirect and usually malicious implication which hints at something damaging to the character or reputation of the person referred to. In *Perspectives on Semantics, Pragmatics, and Discourse*, discourse theorist Bruce Fraser observes that an indirect allegation is encoded in the expression of an innuendo.

For example, the statement 'She is rich, but honest', insinuates that rich people are generally not honest. Similarly, a remark such as 'He was acquitted; it's good to be the son of a politician' implies via innuendo that the father of the accused made corrupt use of his political power to get his guilty son acquitted.

In *The Rape of the Lock*, Pope does something similar in the following lines:

> The hungry judges soon the sentence sign,
> And wretches hang that jury-men may dine.

Pope is indirectly condemning the callous attitudes of judges and members of the jury who irresponsibly hurry through a trial for their own selfish reasons, without considering the implications of their acts on the lives of the accused.

At the end of the third act of Shakespeare's *Macbeth*, Lennox discusses the recent spate of high-profile murders in Scotland with a nobleman. His speech is couched in innuendos.

> ...The gracious Duncan
> Was pitied of Macbeth; marry, he was dead.
> And the right-valiant Banquo walked too late,
> Whom, you may say, if't please you, Fleance kill'd,
> For Fleance fled. Men must not walk too late.

Lennox is indirectly implying that their king, Macbeth, is behind these murders, and his speech reveals that the people of Scotland have begun to see through Macbeth's lies.

Erving Goffman, the renowned sociologist, argues that innuendo and other doublespeak are a kind of 'unofficial' communication where the recipients have to interpret the message for themselves. The 'language of innuendo' is such that the speaker does not give out that he is saying one thing while conveying something else, while the recipient may pretend that he has not received and understood the intended hidden message. Innuendo, therefore, is 'deniable communication' which abdicates any responsibility attached to it.

Take another look at the above example from *Macbeth*. The atmosphere of fear created by Macbeth's reign necessitates that allegations against the powerful tyrant must be made using innuendos. The intended message is only hinted at, but clear. And, if the listener turns out to be Macbeth's spy, the speaker will have deniability, as he has not made a direct or overt statement.

Shakespeare frequently uses **sexual innuendo**, which is the use of words with double meaning, one innocent and one having a sexual implication. This was a very prominent literary figure until about the nineteenth century, when the Victorian emphasis on sexual restraint and morality made such innuendos taboo. (In 1807, Thomas Bowdler published *The Family Shakespeare* which deleted sexual innuendos that were considered 'objectionable'. Subsequently, 'bowdlerise' became a verb meaning 'to edit by deleting or modifying parts of a work considered improper or offensive'.) Examples of the notorious innuendos used by Shakespeare may be found in the following passage from *Hamlet*, where Hamlet is teasing Ophelia:

HAMLET	Lady, shall I lie in your lap?
OPHELIA	No, my lord.
HAMLET	I mean, my head upon your lap?
OPHELIA	Ay, my lord.
HAMLET	Do you think I meant country matters?
OPHELIA	I think nothing, my lord.
HAMLET	That's a fair thought to lie between maids' legs.
OPHELIA	What is, my lord?
HAMLET	Nothing.

'Lie' can mean 'sleep with'. Ophelia is aware of the double meaning. 'Do you think I meant country matters?' would, on one level, mean 'Do you think I meant to be rude and indecent?'; but there is an innuendo in that line as well. Hamlet's use of the words 'head', 'country' and 'nothing' are all references to genitalia, and thus examples of sexual innuendo.

The libel laws of the eighteenth century tolerated innuendo in literature, making it an important weapon in the age of satire. The innuendos found in Pope and Dryden are often political and cultural, which, unlike sexual innuendos, require knowledge of the contemporary socio-political milieu to be fully understood. For example, in *Imitations of Horace*, Pope advises the reader to steer clear of three people he deems vicious:

> Slander or poison dread from Delia's rage;
> Hard words or hanging, if your judge be Page;
> From furious Sappho scarce a milder fate,
> Pox'd by her love, or libell'd by her hate.

Pope's lines have a number of indirect and malicious implications. Delia and Sappho are fictitious names, but contemporary readers would have easily recognised the targets. The first line refers to Lady Deloraine, who was thought to have poisoned another lady. The second innuendo is aimed at Sir Francis Page, a particularly severe judge who was infamous for sentencing several men to death. The last two lines use three innuendos to mock Lady Mary Wortley Montagu. The name 'Sappho' refers to her alleged attraction towards her own sex. 'Pox'd' refers to her loss of beauty after she contracted smallpox, and also to her clandestine affair with a French lover (smallpox was called the 'French disease' in Pope's time). 'Libell'd' refers to Pope's suspicion that Lady Mary wrote some verses to attack Pope. Thus, a lot of background knowledge is required to understand a cultural or political innuendo. It is possibly the most ephemeral of rhetorical figures: much of its meaning is lost to future audiences.

Guided exercise

Find the innuendo in the following passages and explain the doublespeak .

1. Thou blind fool love, what dost thou to mine eyes,
   That they behold, and see not what they see?
   They know what beauty is, see where it *lies*,
   Yet what the best is take the worst to be.
   If eyes corrupt by over-partial looks

Be *anchored in the bay where all men ride,*
Why of eyes' falsehood hast thou forgèd hooks,
Whereto the judgment of my heart is tied?
Why should my heart think that a *several plot*
Which my heart knows *the wide world's common place*?
(Shakespeare, 'Sonnet 137')

2. COUNTESS   Have you, I say, an answer of such fitness for all
              questions?

    CLOWN   *From below your duke to beneath your constable, it
              will fit* any question.

    COUNTESS   It must be an answer of *most monstrous size* that
              must fit all demands.

    (Shakespeare, *All's Well that Ends Well*)

3. *Graze* on my lips, and if those hills be dry
    Stray lower, where *the pleasant fountains* lie.
    (Shakespeare, 'Venus and Adonis')

4. Oh, hadst thou, cruel! been content to *seize*
    Hairs less in sight, or any hairs but these!
    (Pope, *The Rape of the Lock*)

5. 'What do you think of this painting?'
    'Well... *the frame is quite beautiful...*'

IRONY

According to the first-century Roman orator Quintilian, irony is
a rhetorical device that uses words to mean something opposite
to their literal meaning. The classical rhetoricians viewed irony
as one of the four master tropes (the other three being metaphor,
metonymy and synecdoche), as it enriches meaning by a turn of
phrase.

The reader should note that here we will be discussing **verbal
irony**, the proper subject of rhetoric. The other two kinds that
one comes across in literature are *dramatic irony* and *situational
irony*. Both evoke situations where expectations and outcomes are
shockingly incongruous. In verbal irony, we deal with language—
with sentences, not situations. However, the element of incongruity
is present here as well: the *intended* meaning and attitude disagrees
with the literal meaning and the surface attitude.

For example, if someone delivers a rambling and tedious speech, and we refer to it as a short and pertinent lecture, we use irony. If you are late for an appointment but stuck in traffic, and you say 'Great! This is exactly what I needed right now', you are being ironic (because it is understood that you mean the opposite of what you are saying). Irony, therefore, is the opposite of a literal utterance, and the tone of the speaker, as well as the familiar nature of the subject, help to point out the equivocal nature of the ironic expression. Irony is cerebral point-scoring, and it takes a certain measure of intelligence to appreciate an ironical statement.

An excellent example of verbal irony may be found in the opening line of Austen's *Pride and Prejudice*:

It is a truth universally acknowledged that a single man in possession of a good fortune must be in want of a wife.

The sentence is ironic because Austen is implying the opposite: it is actually the nineteenth-century single woman who is in want of a man with a good fortune. In Orwell's *Animal Farm*, the dictatorial Napoleon exiles a fellow leader so that he can enjoy more power. The justification for his act uses verbal irony:

I trust that every animal here appreciates the sacrifice that Comrade Napoleon has made in taking this extra labour upon himself. Do not imagine that leadership is a pleasure.

The names of the branches of the government in Orwell's *Nineteen Eighty-Four* are also instances of verbal irony: the Ministry of Truth spreads propaganda and false dogma; the Ministry of Peace wages war; and the Ministry of Love uses fear, repression and torture to achieve its aims.

Rhetorical irony depends on the distance between what is said and what the narrator (or the author) means to say. Mock epics rely on this distance, and as a result they have grave and sober comments which do not mean what they say. For example, Pope begins *The Rape of the Lock* with an ironical comment:

What dire offence from am'rous causes springs,
What mighty contests rise from trivial things.

'Mighty contests' ironically refers to a petty quarrel between two upper-class families, ensuing from the shearing of a lady's curl of hair by a young nobleman. Eighteenth-century literature has made ample use of irony as a deflating strategy. There was a subsequent period of lesser visibility as Romantic literature introduced serious and sublime ideas. However, there were moments of sabotage when the grand Romantic quest would be reiterated with a faint mockery in the narrative voice, as in these lines from Byron's *Don Juan*:

> Young Juan wander'd by the glassy brooks
> Thinking unutterable things; he threw
> Himself at length within the leafy nooks
> Where the wild branch of the cork forest grew;
> There poets find materials for their books,
> And every now and then we read them through,
> So that their plan and prosody are eligible,
> Unless, like Wordsworth, they prove unintelligible.

This kind of irony undercutting the Romantic sublime is appropriately called 'Romantic irony'.

Ironic mockery can be harmless fun. In his essay 'Quis desiderio...?', Samuel Butler compares the loss of a book with the loss of Lucy, a beloved woman in Wordsworth's ballads:

> All I know is that the book is gone, and I feel as Wordsworth is generally supposed to have felt when he became aware that Lucy was in her grave, and exclaimed so emphatically that this would make a considerable difference to him, or words to that effect ... Lucy was not particularly attractive either inside or out—no more was Frost's *Lives of Eminent Christians*; there were few to praise her, and of those few, still fewer could bring themselves to like her...

Irony became the weapon of the War poets who wished to distance themselves from the chivalric ideals of their contemporary culture and write the poetry of disillusionment. The title of Sassoon's poem 'The Hero' is ironic: the poem recounts the celebrated martyrdom of a clumsy boy who was obliterated at the war front. A similar verbal irony can be found in Wallace Stevens's 'Phases'. Outwardly conforming to chivalric ideals, the poem's lines actually criticise them. Reflecting on the 'heroic' sacrifice of a fallen soldier, the poet asks the reader what an ordinary life could possibly have given the dead soldier in return for the 'salty, sacrificial taste' of 'glory'—a question that reminds us of the potential wasted by the needless death.

A dry ironic tone marks the poetry of T.S. Eliot and his contemporaries in the twentieth century. The narrator of Eliot's 'Portrait of a Lady' refers to the tastefully arranged parlour of an upper-middle-class lady as having the 'atmosphere of Juliet's tomb'. Such use of irony allows the narrator to distance himself from the situation, but also damages all efforts to arrive at a moment of earnestness.

Irony is often used as a political device to attack and expose complacent points of view. As great writers have shown us many times, irony can be a powerful rhetorical device to subvert accepted 'truths' that have become so ingrained in our society and our way of thinking that speaking plainly against them is not enough.

Guided exercise

Explain the figure of speech in the lines given below.

1. No doubt but ye are the people, and *wisdom shall die with you.*
   (The Book of Job)

2. Last Week I saw a Woman flay'd, and you will hardly believe, *how much it altered her Person for the Worse.*
   (Swift, *A Tale of a Tub*)

3. Now lap-dogs give themselves the rousing shake,
   And *sleepless lovers, just at twelve, awake*
   (Pope, *The Rape of the Lock*)

   The romantic cliché of 'sleepless lovers' is undercut by the ironic fact of them waking up from sleep at noon.

4. But Brutus says he was ambitious,
   And *Brutus is an honourable man.* (Shakespeare, *Julius Caesar*)

5. And *I say his opinion was good.*
   Why should he study, and make himself wood
   Upon a book in cloister always pore,
   Or swinken with his hands, *and labour,*
   As Austin bid? *How shall the world be served?*
   (Chaucer, *The Canterbury Tales*)

   The narrator outwardly endorses the lifestyle of the monk who was given to wordly pleasures, while reminding us of the duties of a true monk.

6. ... *the progress of science* cannot, perhaps, be otherwise registered than *by new facilities of destruction*; and the *brotherly love* of our enlarging Christianity be only *proved by multiplication of murder* (Ruskin, *The Crown of Wild Olive*)

SARCASM

Sarcasm is intentional derision and verbal aggression usually involving overt irony. It may be used to taunt or hurt a person or a group of people, or even attack an idea. It uses language in such a way as to excite contempt or ridicule. In speech, sarcasm is commonly indicated by inflecting one's voice (that is, altering the tone and pitch of the voice).

In Marvell's 'To His Coy Mistress', the frustrated lover mocks his overly modest beloved for rejecting his advances:

> The grave is a fine and private place
> But none I think do there embrace.

His caustic comments ridicule her cold chastity. Sarcasm thus makes use of keen reproachful expressions, usually accompanied by some degree of scorn.

In Shakespeare's *Twelfth Night*, the short-statured Maria makes fun of the protagonist Viola, who in turn retaliates by sarcastically referring to Maria as a 'giant'. In *Julius Caesar*, Cassius is annoyed that the people of Rome fawn upon Caesar as though he were a god. He recounts an incident when Caesar had an epileptic fit, saying:

> 'Tis true, this god did shake!

Cassius is sneering at Caesar: a god wouldn't suffer from epilepsy, and so Caesar is no god. (This line also works as an innuendo.)

When Hamlet, feigning madness, tells Ophelia that his father has been dead for less than two hours, she corrects him, saying that it has been four months in fact. Hamlet's reply is dripping with sarcasm:

> So long? ... O heavens! die two months ago and not forgotten yet? Then there's hope a great man's memory may outlive his life half a year.

The bitterness in these lines expresses Hamlet's deep sorrow and anger at his mother's hasty marriage to his uncle after the death of his father.

Sarcasm and irony

These two terms are closely related, though one must not be mistaken for the other. Irony highlights the underlying absurdity of something. Irony may be used to create humour, to mock someone, or to simply comment on something. Sarcasm, however, is always used for mockery—usually to intentionally hurt someone.

In verbal irony, what is said is contrary to what is meant. Sarcasm often uses irony (an indirect attack), but sometimes expresses contempt directly and plainly (without recourse to irony). Let us see a simple example of this from *Pride and Prejudice*. Mrs Bennet insists that her family attend a party so that she may introduce her unmarried daughters to the rich bachelor Bingley. Mr Bennet mocks his wife by saying:

> ... as you are as handsome as any of them, Mr Bingley might like you the best of the party.

Mr Bennet is being sarcastic, and he uses irony as the vehicle for his sarcasm. He does not genuinely believe that Bingley will find his wife attractive. Mrs Bennet replies that at her age, she must not think of her own beauty. Again, Mr Bennet responds with sarcasm:

> In such cases a woman has not often much beauty to think of.

This time, however, Mr Bennet is bluntly saying that his wife is no longer beautiful. There is no irony in this instance of sarcasm.

Guided exercise

Explain the figure of speech in the lines given below.

1. God has not been so sparing to men to make them barely two-legged creatures, and *left it to Aristotle to make them rational* (Locke, *Of Human Understanding*)

2. You would *pet him, and spoil him, and mother him to perfection.* (Shaw, *Arms and the Man*)

3. Is not *a patron,* My Lord, *one who looks with unconcern on a man struggling for life in the water, and when he has reached ground, encumbers him with help?* (Johnson, 'Letter to Chesterfield')

4. *Some soldiers*, I know, *are afraid of death.*
    (Shaw, *Arms and the Man*)

5. Christianity does not mean *carrying the cross on the bosom and crucifying Christ at every step.*

6. *I fear I wrong the honourable men*
    Whose daggers have stabb'd Caesar. (Shakespeare, *Julius Caesar*)

7. Rejoice, young man, during your childhood, and let your heart be pleasant during the days of young manhood. And follow the impulses of your heart and the desires of your eyes. Yet know that *God will bring you to judgment for all these things.* (Ecclesiastes)

8. Reader, suppose you were an idiot. And suppose you were a member of Congress. But *I repeat myself.* (Mark Twain)

PERIPHRASIS OR CIRCUMLOCUTION

This figure consists in stating something not directly but in a roundabout way. The laconic nature of direct speech usually lacks semantic richness. Periphrasis often adds depth and magnificence to the language of poetry. Consider the following lines from Shakespeare's 'Sonnet 74':

> ... when that fell arrest
> Without all bail shall carry me away

The expression 'fell [cruel] arrest / Without all bail' means 'death' in plain English. Death takes one into custody as if with a non-bailable arrest warrant. The legal images in the circumlocution convey a sense of helplessness and finality from which one cannot escape ('arrest / Without all bail'). This richness of meaning is absent in the simple word 'death'.

Periphrasis was a staple device of epic and descriptive poetry from classical times to the Renaissance. Consider the following instance from Spenser's *Faerie Queene*:

> And whilst he bath'd, with her two crafty spyes,
> She secretly would search each dainty lim.

'Eyes' are described as 'two crafty spies'. Such periphrasis adds meaning: the woman's gaze is surreptitious; like a spy, she observes him but takes care to be discreet.

This kind of circumlocutory language became increasingly popular in neoclassical verse. Simple, direct words and phrases were deemed 'unpoetic', and hence elaborate and 'elegant' phrases were contrived as substitutes. A major element of eighteenth-century style was the invention of vivid, periphrastic diction to describe trivial things (for example, 'the fatal engine' for a pair of scissors in Pope's *The Rape of the Lock*). The sense of artificiality this gave to language led some scholars, such as A.C. Partridge, to describe periphrasis as one of the 'vices' of. Augustan expression (*The Language of Renaissance Poetry*).

The early Romantics rejected the complex sophisticated expressions of Augustan poetry in favour of simpler language inspired by rural life. However, periphrasis is not uncommon in Romantic poetry. Consider this example from *The Lady of the Lake* by Sir Walter Scott, in which a man's body is imagined as a clay burial cloth endowed with consciousness.:

> For man endowed with mortal life,
> Whose shroud of sentient clay can still
> Feel feverish pang and fainting chill

A famous example of periphrasis in Victorian literature may be found in Dickens's *David Copperfield*. The following passage, in which Mr Micawber gives directions to the protagonist, conforms to the Augustan model of grand circumlocution to achieve a comic effect:

> 'Under the impression', said Mr. Micawber, 'that your peregrinations in this metropolis have not as yet been extensive, and that you might have some difficulty in penetrating the arcana of the Modern Babylon in the direction of the City Road—in short', said Mr. Micawber, ... 'that you might lose yourself—I shall be happy to call this evening, and install you in the knowledge of the nearest way.'

In Tennyson's *Morte d'Arthur*, massive, cold icebergs are described as large floating islands of permanent winter:

> Seen where the moving isles of winter shock
> By night, with noises of the northern sea.

Speaking in a roundabout way helps to dramatise the situation and inspire awe. This function still retains its place of importance in literature, even in the twentieth century, when language has become increasingly terse, curt and ironic.

Guided exercise

Explain the figure of speech in the lines given below.

1. The *sleep that knows no waking* (= death)
2. The *shining leather that encases the limb* (= boot)
3. the *cups / That cheer but not inebriate* (Cowper, *The Task*) (= tea)
4. the *sightless couriers of air* (Shakespeare, *Macbeth*) (= winds)
5. That *orbed maiden with white fire laden* (Shelley, 'The Cloud') (= the moon)

EUPHEMISM

This figure consists in making a disagreeable statement seem agreeable through inoffensive or indirect expression. A euphemism substitutes a harsh expression with a mild one, or softens the harsh word or expression. To make something offensive palatable, one often needs to put it in a roundabout way. As a result, euphemisms often make use of circumlocution.

> He could not satisfy his examiner. (= He could not clear the test.)

Euphemism and periphrasis

There is some difference between euphemism and periphrasis, although both are roundabout statements. In euphemism, the indirect statement is made to soften a harsh statement, whereas in periphrasis, it is done only for literary effect.

When Shakespeare periphrastically describes death as 'that fell arrest / Without all bail', he is being indirect in order to make his lines more poetic by adding beauty and depth. When we euphemistically say someone 'passed away' (to mean that the person died), we are being indirect in order to avoid sounding blunt when referring to something unpleasant.

Euphemism and innuendo

Both euphemism and innuendo refer to something in an indirect manner. The difference, once again, is one of intent. An (non-sexual) innuendo is often prompted by a hostile feeling: it wants to hurt. A euphemism, on the other hand, is prompted by a kindly feeling: it wants to spare.

Guided exercise

Explain the figure of speech in the lines given below.

1. She has *not stated the truth.* (= lied)

2. She *breathed her last.* (= died)

3. He *died on the scaffold.* (= was hanged)

4. He is *short in his accounts.* (= poor)

5. The *light-fingered gentlemen* of trams and buses (= pickpockets)

6. A *terminological inexactitude* (= lie)

7. He's *safe with gentle Jesus!* (Galsworthy, *Justice*) (= dead)

8. To *relieve a person of* his money bag (= rob)

MEIOSIS

This figure consists in making an understatement. The effect is usually ironic or **anticlimactic** (see page 58). Consider the following exchange from Shakespeare's *Romeo and Juliet* after Mercutio is mortally wounded:

MERCUTIO	Ay, ay, a scratch, a scratch. Marry, 'tis enough. Where is my page?—Go, villain, fetch a surgeon.
ROMEO	Courage, man; the hurt cannot be much.
MERCUTIO	No, 'tis not so deep as a well, nor so wide as a church-door; but 'tis enough, 'twill serve ...

Mercutio refers to a mortal gash as a 'scratch' which, though neither deep nor wide, is enough to kill a person. Mark the ironical tone of his statement.

LITOTES

Litotes (pronounced *lie-toe-teez*, with the stress on the first syllable) is a type of understatement in which something is affirmed by denying the contrary. Litotes is regularly found in common speech. Saying 'I was not a little upset' to mean 'I was very upset' is an example of litotes. In the same way, 'He is a citizen of no mean city' means that he is the resident of a large or important city.

Consider the following passage from Milton's *Paradise Lost*:

> Into this wild Abyss the warie fiend
> Stood on the brink of Hell and look'd a while,
> Pondering his Voyage: for no narrow frith
> He had to cross. Nor was his eare less peal'd
> With noises loud and ruinous ...

Milton means to say that Satan had to cross a really huge estuary, and that his ears were resounding with deafening sounds. These extreme conditions are conveyed through a denial of the contrary ('no narrow' and 'less peal'd').

Guided exercise

Explain the figure of speech in the lines given below.

1. Much have I seen and known; cities of men
   And manners, climates, councils, governments,
   Myself *not least*, but honour'd of them all (Tennyson, 'Ulysses')
   = the foremost

2. The culprit was indeed *not unworthy* of that great presence.
   (Macaulay, 'Warren Hastings')
   = quite worthy

3. *No maiden's hand* is around thee thrown
   (Scott, *The Lady of the Lake*)
   = a powerful man's hand

4. Some work of noble note, may yet be done,
   Not unbecoming men that strove with Gods.
   (Tennyson, 'Ulysses')
   = most becoming/worthy

5. I hope it is *no very cynical asperity* not to confess obligations where no benefit has been received.
   (Johnson, 'Letter to Chesterfield')
   = entirely justified and proportionate

6. *Not a few men* came to see Nehru.
   = many men

7. His *not unworthy, not inglorious* son.
   (Arnold, 'Sohrab and Rustum')
   = worthy and glorious

8. It amused the King *not a little.*
   = a lot

SIX

Figures based on Emotion

INTERROGATION OR EROTESIS

It is a figure of speech in the form of a question where no answer is expected by the speaker as the answer is obvious. This is a rhetorical question where the enquirer knows what answer he will get.

Here is an example from Shakespeare's *The Merchant of Venice*:

> ... what's his reason? I am a Jew. Hath not a Jew eyes? hath not a Jew hands, organs, dimensions, senses, affections, passions? fed with the same food, hurt with the same weapons, subject to the same diseases, healed by the same means, warmed and cooled by the same winter and summer, as a Christian is? If you prick us, do we not bleed? if you tickle us, do we not laugh? if you poison us, do we not die? and if you wrong us, shall we not revenge?

In the above passage, a series of questions with self-evident answers follow the speaker's assertion that he has been discriminated against due to his ethnicity. These questions are not really questions but emotional reminders of the commonness of humanity.

Let us take another example, from Gray's 'Elegy Written in a Country Churchyard':

> Can storied urn or animated bust
> Back to its mansion call the fleeting breath?
> Can Honour's voice provoke the silent dust,
> Or Flatt'ry soothe the dull cold ear of Death?

A journey backwards from ashes to life is not possible. The questions are not asked in order to seek answers, but rather to make an emotional assertion of the finality of death.

Guided exercise

Explain the figure of speech in the lines given below.

1. *Can the Ethiopian change his skin, or the leopard his spots?*
   (Jeremiah, 'The Book of Jeremiah')

2. But *why ... should we care about the opinion of the many?*
   (Socrates, Plato's *Crito*)

3. I thrice presented him a kingly crown which he did thrice refuse: *Was this ambition?* (Shakespeare, *Julius Caesar*)

   The question is not an inquiry, but an impassioned reminder to the audience that this was *not* ambition.

4. *Who is here so vile that will not love his country?*
   (Shakespeare, *Julius Caesar*)

   Such questions with obvious answers can be very useful in a political speech. Nobody will rise up and declare himself 'so vile [as to] not love his country'—the orator thus establishes his control over the audience.

5. *Who is here so base that would be a bondman?*
   (Shakespeare, *Julius Caesar*)

   A similar rhetorical ploy is used to secure control over the audience.

6. O Wind, / *If Winter comes, can Spring be far behind?*
   (Shelley, 'Ode to the West Wind')

   The question evokes hope for the future.

7. *Is this the region, this the soil, the clime,*
   Said then the lost arch-angel, *this the seat*
   That we must change for Heav'n, this mournful gloom
   For that celestial light? (Milton, *Paradise Lost*)

   Satan confirms to his archangels that after their fall they must accept the space of purgatory in exchange of the luminous grounds of heaven. These questions are not seeking information, but are instead an emotional acceptance of the present situation.

8. *Fail I alone, in words and deeds?*
   Why, all men strive and *who succeeds?*
   (Browning, 'The Last Ride Together')

The speaker asks two successive questions which underscore the futility of ambition.

9. *For who would bear the whips and scorns of time,*
   The oppressor's wrong, the proud man's contumely,
   The pangs of despis'd love, the law's delay,
   The insolence of office, and the spurns
   That patient merit of th' unworthy takes,
   When he himself might his quietus make
   With a bare bodkin? Who would these fardels bear,
   To grunt and sweat under a weary life,
   But that the dread of something after death,
   The undiscover'd country, from whose bourn
   No traveller returns, puzzles the will,
   And makes us rather bear those ills we have
   Than fly to others that we know not of? (Shakespeare, *Hamlet*)

10. *And is this Yarrow?* This the stream
    Of which my fancy cherish'd
    So faithfully, a waking dream,
    An image that hath perish'd? (Wordsworth, 'Yarrow Visited')

    The first question is a simple erotesis, while the second contains two other figures that are highlighted in grey. Can you recognise them? (Refer to Chapters 3 and 4.)

11. Gods! *shall the ravisher display your hair,*
    While the fops envy, and the ladies stare!
    (Pope, *The Rape of the Lock*)

12. *Shall we receive good at the hand of God,*
    And evil not receive? (Browning, 'The Melon-Seller')

EXCLAMATION

The exclamation is an abrupt emphatic expression of an emotion, contemplation or wish. An exclamation is typically introduced by simple interjections such as 'Oh!' or exclamatory expressions such as 'O what a—', 'O how—', 'But O—', and so on. See, for example, the following excerpt from Shakespeare's *Hamlet*:

> What a piece of work is a man! how noble in reason! how infinite in faculty! in form and moving how express and

admirable! in action how like an angel! in apprehension how like a god! the beauty of the world! the paragon of animals!

Here we have a series of exclamations (a total of eight) which express Hamlet's deep contemplation on the nature of human life, and his resulting sense of wonder. The expressions are mostly introduced by 'what' and 'how', and sometimes without interjections. 'The beauty of the world' actually means 'Nothing in the world is more beautiful than man!' Introductory interjections may be dropped towards the end of a series.

The following passage, from Keats's 'Ode to a Nightingale', has two famous instances of exclamation:

> O for a draught of vintage! that hath been
> Cool'd a long age in the deep-delvèd earth,
> Tasting of Flora and the country-green,
> Dance, and Provençal song, and sunburnt mirth!
> O for a beaker full of the warm South!

Through these exclamations, Keats abruptly expresses his intense desire for a cup of rich Provençal wine.

Guided exercise

Explain the figure of speech in the lines given below.

1. *But O for the touch of a vanished hand,*
   And the sound of a voice that is still!
   (Tennyson, 'Break, Break, Break')

   An abrupt expression of a wish to see a dead person again

2. *How sweet the moonlight sleeps upon this bank!*
   (Shakespeare, *The Merchant of Venice*)

   An emotional response to natural beauty, introduced by an exclamatory expression

3. *Gun upon gun, ha! ha! / Gun upon gun, hurrah!*
   (Chesterton, 'Lepanto')

   Exclamations rejoicing in the sounds of battle

4. *Oh, our manhood's prime vigour!* No spirit feels waste,
   Not a muscle is stopped in its playing nor sinew unbraced.

Oh, the wild joys of living! the leaping from rock up to rock,
The strong rending of boughs from the fir-tree, the cool silver
  shock
Of the plunge in a pool's living water, the hunt of the bear, ...
And the sleep in the dried river-channel where bulrushes tell
That the water was wont to go warbling so softly and well.
How good is man's life, the mere living! (Browning, 'Saul')

Exultations on the vigour of youth

5.   *... Great God! I'd rather be*
   A pagan suckled in a creed outworn
   (Wordsworth, 'The World is Too Much with Us')

   A protest against the formally Christian but materialist culture
   of the poet's time

6. *Oh had I the wings of a dove,*
   How soon would I taste you again!
   (Cowper, 'The Solitude of Alexander Selkirk')

   An emotional outburst from a shipwrecked speaker who
   mourns the loss of society, friendship and love, and wishes
   desperately to experience them again

7. *O, what a fall was there, my countrymen!*
   (Shakespeare, *Julius Caesar*)

   Lamentation for the loss of a great leader

8. *Oh! That the desert were my dwelling place*
   (Byron, *Childe Harold's Pilgrimage*)

   An exclamation expressing a wish

9. But she is in her grave, and, *oh,*
   The difference to me!
   (Wordsworth, 'She Dwelt Among the Untrodden Ways')

   Lamentation for the death of an unknown girl, whose passing
   does not affect anyone else

SEVEN

Figures based on Construction

HENDIADYS

The term 'hendiadys' (plural: hendiades) was coined by the Latin grammarian Servius (c. 400 CE) to describe a common figure in Virgil's *Aeneid*. Hendiadys expresses an idea through two independent words connected by 'and' (for example, 'nice *and* warm') instead of the usual combination of an independent word with its modifier ('nicely warm'). When two nouns are connected by the conjunction 'and', instead of one modifying the other, they can convey an idea more forcefully than the more common combination of a noun qualified by an adjective. The most famous example of hendiadys is from Virgil's *Georgics*:

We drink from cups and gold.

Here, the usual adjective-noun pair 'golden cups' is replaced by the phrase 'cups and gold'. Some translators deem it an oddity, while other commentators emphasise that Virgil wants the readers to grasp two ideas: the celebratory golden cup is as important as its rich contents. Hendiadys fuses both ideas together. This element of surprise at the bending of grammar, combined with the expression of a complex idea, is the hallmark of hendiadys. It is a prevalent figure in the Bible, as seen in this example from the Book of Genesis:

I will greatly multiply thy sorrow and thy conception

Rather than using an adjective and a noun to describe a single concept, this hendiadic expression joins two nouns with the conjunction 'and'. The expression means 'your pain and your labour', that is, 'your labour pains'.

Hendiadys was frequently used by Shakespeare, especially in *Hamlet* and *Othello*. The first instance of hendiadys in *Hamlet* occurs after Horatio witnesses the murdered king's ghost:

...in the gross and scope of mine opinion
This bodes some strange eruption to our state.

Here 'gross and scope' means 'broad view'. Laertes uses this figure when he asks the new king's permission to return to France:

My dread lord,
Your leave and favour to return to France

The expression means 'kind permission'. Hendiadys marks Macbeth's impassioned speech too:

it is a tale
Told by an idiot, full of sound and fury, [furious sound]
Signifying nothing.

Though primarily involving nouns, hendiadys can also involve other grammatical units such as adjectives and verbs. Look at this example from Sweet's *The Old Chapel*:

Harry Webb lay and sobbed bitterly.

Here, the hendiadic combination 'lay and sobbed' (two verbs) substitutes 'lay sobbing', in which the participle 'sobbing' functions as an adverbial adjunct of 'lay'. Similarly, adjectival hendiadys is fairly common. For example, this passage from *Othello* uses a series of adjectival hendiades to create complex modifiers:

Let her have your voices.
Vouch with me, heaven, I therefore beg it not
To please the palate of my appetite,
Nor to comply with heat—the young affects
In me defunct—and proper satisfaction.
But to be free and bounteous to her mind:
And heaven defend your good souls, that you think
I will your serious and great business scant
For she is with me: no, when light-wing'd toys
Of feather'd Cupid seal with wanton dullness
My speculative and officed instruments,
That my disports corrupt and taint my business,
Let housewives make a skillet of my helm,
And all indign and base adversities
Make head against my estimation!

These hendiadic pairs of adjectives qualify each other and fuse to signify complex ideas. They are not simple adjective pairs like 'She wore a *tall and white* hat', where 'tall' and 'white' separately describe the hat but do not qualify each other or fuse into a complex idea.

Keats's sonnet 'To One Who Has Been Long in City Pent' has three types of hendiades:

> Fatigued he sinks into some pleasant lair
> Of wavy grass, and reads a debonair
> And gentle tale of love and languishment

The first example, 'sinks … and reads' is *verbal hendiadys* meaning 'sinks (into the grass) reading', where the participle (reading) qualifies the preceding verb (sinks) and describes a complex state of peacefulness. Next, 'debonair and gentle' is *adjectival hendiadys*, where two adjectives qualify each other to present a complex idea about a sophisticated yet mellow love-story. Finally, 'love and languishment' is an example of *noun hendiadys*, which emphasises Keats's idea better than the adjective-noun pair 'languishing love'.

Laurie Maguire observes in her book *Othello: Language and Writing* that hendiadys, along with **oxymoron** (page 53) and **paradox** (page 63), are conflating strategies that fuse two incompatibles into one. In this regard, it is different from a figure such as the **pun** (page 127), which deconstructs meaning, expanding one meaning into two.

Guided exercise

The hendiadic pairs are highlighted for you. Try to provide the adjective-noun pair.

1. With *joy and song*
   I clear my way. (Lascelles Abercrombie, 'The Stream's Song')
   = joyful song

2. … his look / Drew *audience and attention* still as Night
   (Milton, *Paradise Lost*)
   = attentive audience

3. … the *trade and profit* of the city
   (Shakespeare, *The Merchant of Venice*)
   = profitable trade

4. ... with *joy* / *And tidings* (Milton, *Paradise Lost*)
   = joyous tidings

5. ... *mysteries and presences* innumerable
   (Ruskin, *The Crown of Wild Olive*)
   = mysterious presences

6. The hall was full of *melody and misses*
   = melodious misses

7. The *heaviness and guilt* within my bosom
   Takes off my manhood (Shakespeare, *Cymbeline*)
   = heavy guilt

8. Fred must *make haste and get well.* (George Eliot, *Middlemarch*)
   = recover quickly

9. *life and sufferance* (Byron, *Childe Harold's Pilgrimage*)
   = suffering life

10. *Perfume and flowers* fall in showers (Tennyson, 'Sir Galahad')
    = fragrant flowers

11. Thou foster-child of *silence and slow time*
    (Keats, 'Ode on a Grecian Urn')
    = silent, slow-moving time

CHIASMUS

Derived from the Greek word for 'crossing', this figure consists in the inversion of the structures of two parallel clauses within a sentence. See, for example, this well-known example from Keats's 'Ode on a Grecian Urn':

> Beauty is truth, truth beauty

Examine the chiastic pattern of the line given above:
- The line has two clauses.
- The structure of the first clause is 'A is B' (beauty is truth).
- The structure of the second clause is 'B is A' (truth is beauty).
- The structure of the second clause is an inversion of the structure of the first clause.

Guided exercise

Explain the figure of speech in the lines given below.

1. And *singing still dost soar*, and *soaring ever singest*.
   (Shelley, 'To a Skylark')

2. I balanced all, brought all to mind,
   The years to come seemed waste of breath,
   A waste of breath the years behind
   In balance with this life, this death.
   (Yeats, 'An Irish Airman Forsees His Death')

3. For *the sky and the sea*, and *the sea and the sky*
   Lay like a load on my weary eye
   (Coleridge, 'The Rime of the Ancient Mariner')
   What other rhetorical devices can you spot in these lines?

4. *Fair is foul*, and *foul is fair* (Shakespeare, *Macbeth*)

5. ... *ask not what your country can do for you—ask what you can
   do for your country*. (Kennedy, 'Inaugural address')

6. 'Let *spades be trumps!*' she said, and *trumps they were*.
   (Pope, *The Rape of the Lock*)

7. *Down dropt the breeze, the sails dropt down*
   (Coleridge, 'The Rime of the Ancient Mariner')

8. *A wit with dunces*, and *a dunce with wits*. (Pope, *The Dunciad*)

9. For *love is heaven*, and *heaven is love*.
   (Scott, 'The Lay of the Last Minstrel')

10. The mind is its own place, and in itself
    Can make *a heaven of hell, a hell of heaven*.
    (Milton, *Paradise Lost*)

ELLIPSIS

Ellipsis (from the Greek word for 'leaving out') is the grammatical
omission of a part of a sentence for the sake of brevity, elegance or
emphasis. Recall, for example, these lines from a popular nursery
rhyme:

Jack fell down
And [...] broke his crown

In the second line, the subject (Jack/he) has been left out because it is understood and because including it would spoil the rhythm of the line.

Look at the following examples from Milton's *Paradise Lost*:

> To thee no reason

The words left out are 'this is': To thee, *this is* no reason.

> Lives there who loves his pain ...?

The words left out are 'a man': Lives there *a man* who loves his pain?

ZEUGMA

Zeugma (derived from the Greek word for 'yoking together') consists in a single verb connecting more than one subject (commonly nouns), object, or clause.

A single verb may connect multiple subjects, as in the following lines from Shakespeare's 'Sonnet 55':

> Not marble nor the gilded monuments
> Of princes shall outlive this powerful rhyme.

A single verb, 'outlive', serves two subjects, 'marble' and 'the gilded monuments of princes'. In the next example from 'Sonnet 73', the verb 'hang' takes multiple subjects (yellow leaves, no leaves, few leaves):

> That time of year thou may'st in me behold
> When yellow leaves, or none, or few, do hang
> Upon those boughs which shake against the cold

A single verb may connect multiple objects, as in the following lines from Shakespeare's 'Sonnet 128':

> Give them thy fingers, me thy lips to kiss.

A single verb may serve more than one clause, as illustrated by the following example from Shakespeare's *Romeo and Juliet*:

> But passion lends them power, time means, to meet

Here we have two clauses: 'passion lends them the power (ability) to meet' and 'time lends them the means (ways) to meet'. The verb 'lends', which serves both clauses has been left out of the second clause. In the next example, taken from Shakespeare's 'Sonnet 91', one verb ('glory', meaning 'to rejoice') serves multiple clauses:

> Some glory in their birth, some in their skill,
> Some in their wealth, some in their body's force,
> Some in their garments, though new-fangled ill;
> Some in their hawks and hounds, some in their horse;
> And every humour hath his adjunct pleasure,
> Wherein it finds a joy above the rest

In classical Greek and Latin literature, the term 'zeugma' was reserved for a specific construction in which a word applies to two others even though it semantically suits only one. That is, in the zeugma, the single word seems logically connected to only one of the two nouns/subjects, and does not actually make proper sense with the other one. Examine the following line from Pope's 'Windsor Forest':

> See Pan with flocks, with fruits Pomona crowned

A single verb, 'crowned', is applied to Pan (Greek god of shepherds) and Pomona (Roman goddess of fruitful abundance). It makes sense for Pomona to be 'crowned' with fruits, but the image of Pan 'crowned' with sheep makes less sense. The zeugma allows a writer to use a word in a narrower as well as a wider sense. The reader understands what the writer means and supplies the appropriate word: Pan is *surrounded* by flocks. Another example of this classical form of zeugma may be found in Shakespeare's *Henry V*:

> Kill the poys [boys] and the luggage!

Two nouns ('boys' and 'luggage') are yoked forcefully together with the same verb ('kill'), even though the verb is strictly appropriate to only one of them—the speaker means 'kill the boys' and '*destroy/plunder* the luggage'.

Zeugma and syllepsis (condensed sentence)

In Latin and Greek, the terms 'syllepsis' and 'zeugma' had distinct meanings and functions. The two terms were imported into English from classical literature, but the grammar of 20th-century English caused an overlap between them. Over the years, some English grammarians and rhetoricians attempted to keep these two terms distinct; other grammarians used one or the other term for *both* the classical senses; and yet others resorted to using the name 'condensed sentence' as a broad term for the structure created as a result of using syllepsis/zeugma.

As a result of this, much confusion has arisen regarding the use of these terms. Some rhetoricians have placed zeugma under syllepsis, and vice versa. Syllepsis and zeugma are now often used as synonyms for each other. The term 'condensed sentence' began life as a combined name for both syllepsis and zeugma, although now it is mostly applied to syllepsis alone.

Both syllepsis and zeugma involve ellipses: they omits words—usually verbs—for rhetorical impact. The zeugma is used for dramatic effect. Here is an example from Scott's *Marmion*:

> Would hide her wrongs, and her revenge

As noted a little earlier, zeugma is also used for constructions that may be semantically inappropriate (although grammatically correct). Here, too, the effect is serious, as in this line from Byron's *Childe Harold's Pilgrimage*:

> Banners on high and battles passed below

In these lines, the verbs 'hide' and 'passed' are *not* used in two different senses, nor is there any grammatical error (even if the word is not always the most appropriate one).

Now examine the following lines from Pope's *The Rape of the Lock*:

> Here thou, great Anna! whom three realms obey,
> Dost sometimes counsel take—and sometimes tea.

Here, just as in zeugma, one verb ('take') connects two nouns ('counsel' and 'tea'). However, this is an instance of syllepsis: the verb 'take' is used in *two different senses*—'receive (advice)' and 'drink (tea)'. The connected nouns/ideas are so different that the yoking together is absurd and the result, unlike that of a zeugma, is hilarious. A satirical strain, the hallmark of syllepsis, is evident here.

Guided exercise

Explain the figure of speech in the lines printed on the next page. The verbs are highlighted for you.

1. She saw him not: and while he stood on deck
   Waving, the moment and the vessel *past.*
   (Tennyson, 'Enoch Arden')

2. He *held* a cross on the bosom and a revolver in the hand.

3. Lust *conquered* shame; audacity, fear; madness, reason.
   (Cicero, *Pro Cluentio*)

4. Histories *make* men wise; poets, witty; the mathematics, subtle;
   natural philosophy, deep; moral, grave; logic and rhetoric, able
   to contend. (Bacon, 'Of Studies')

5. Can the Ethiopian *change* his skin, or the leopard his spots?
   (The Book of Jeremiah)

6. For contemplation he and valour *formed,*
   For softness she and sweet attractive grace
   (Milton, *Paradise Lost*)

   He was formed (made) for contemplation and valour; she was
   formed for softness and grace.

POLYSYNDETON AND ASYNDETON

Syndeton refers to the connection of words, phrases or clauses
using a conjunction.

> He bought <u>a packet of biscuits</u>, <u>some sweets</u>, <u>a newspaper</u>
> *and* <u>a bottle of water</u>.

In the above sentence, all the items the person bought are connected
with commas, and the conjunction 'and' signals the end of the list.
Both polysyndeton and asyndeton flout this rule to create a vivid
impression.

Polysyndeton (*poly* = 'many') consists in the excessive use of
conjunctions in close succession. It slows down the pace of a line,
and either creates a sense of breathless abundance or forces the
reader to pay attention to each item in the list. See, for example the
following example of polysyndeton in Tennyson's 'Ulysses':

> That hoard, and sleep, and feed, and know not me.

Without polysyndeton, the line would read 'That hoard, sleep,
feed, *and* know not me'. Here is another example of polysyndeton
from the book of Genesis:

And they come in unto the place of which God hath spoken to him, and there Abraham buildeth the altar, and arrangeth the wood, and bindeth Isaac his son, and placeth him upon the altar above the wood; and Abraham putteth forth his hand, and taketh the knife—to slaughter his son.

Asyndeton (*a* = 'without') removes conjunctions and uses only commas. If Tennyson had written the above line from 'Ulysses' asyndetically, it would have read 'That hoard, sleep, feed, know not me'. Asyndeton speeds up the pace of a line, emphasising the relation between the items in a list. Take a look at the following example of asyndeton from Shakespeare's *Julius Caesar*:

O mighty Caesar! Dost thou lie so low?
Are all thy conquests, glories, triumphs, spoils,
Shrunk to this little measure?

Guided exercise

Explain the figure of speech in the lines given below.

1. I bought *fish and meat and vegetables and chillies and oranges and sweets.*

2. Neither *blindness, nor gout, nor age, nor penury, nor domestic afflictions, nor political disappointments, nor abuse, nor prescription, nor neglect* had power to disturb his sedate and majestic patience. (Macaulay, 'Milton')

3. Theirs be *the music, the colour, the glory, the gold* (Masefield, 'A Consecration')

4. *I slip, I slide, I gloom, I glance* (Tennyson, 'The Brook')

5. What a noble mind is here overthrown!
The *courtier's, soldier's, scholar's, eye, tongue, sword* (Shakespeare, *Hamlet*)

6. The ice was all around:
It *cracked and growled, and roared and howled,*
Like noises in a swound!
(Coleridge, 'The Rime of the Ancient Mariner')

See also **onomatopoeia**, page 130.

7. Souls that have *toil'd, and wrought, and thought* with me (Tennyson, 'Ulysses')

8. From Art more various are the blessings sent—
   Wealth, commerce, honour, liberty, content.
   (Goldsmith, 'The Traveller')

9. *A speck, a mist, a shape*, I wist!
   And still it neared and neared:
   As if it dodged a water-sprite,
   It *plunged and tacked and veered.*
   (Coleridge, 'The Rime of the Ancient Mariner')

HYPERBATON OR INVERSION

Hyperbaton (Greek for 'overstepping') consists in the inversion or transposition of the normal grammatical order of words in a sentence for the sake of emphasis. Some elements of the regular syntax *overstep* others. Let us take an example from Milton's *Paradise Lost* to understand how it works.

Him the Almighty Power
Hurl'd headlong flaming from th' Ethereal Sky

English syntax follows the order: subject–verb–complement–modifier. In regular English, the above sentence would have been:

the Almighty Power	Hurl'd	Him	headlong ...
SUBJECT	VERB	COMPLEMENT	MODIFIERS

Milton's irregular syntax (complement–subject–verb: Him | the Almighty Power | hurl'd) would sound foreign to a native English speaker. Latin and its daughter languages (such as French) have flexible syntax like this. (They are sister languages of Sanskrit and other Indian languages.) Milton deliberately used Latin syntax in English to create a sense of strangeness or other-worldliness. Here is another example from *Paradise Lost*:

Him who disobeys, me disobeys

The usual English syntax would be:

who	disobeys	Him,	disobeys	me
SUBJECT	VERB	COMPLEMENT	VERB	COMPLEMENT

However, Milton uses hyperbaton to transgress this word order:

Him	who	disobeys,	me	disobeys
COMPLEMENT	SUBJECT	VERB	COMPLEMENT	VERB
	Relative clause		Main clause	

The Latinate hyperbaton often results in a kind of quaintness. See, for example, the following use of hyperbaton from the Acts of the Apostles in the *King James Bible*:

> Peter said, Silver and gold have I none; but such as I have give I thee ...

Clearly, functional English syntax is broken here in this translation from Latin. If we compare it to the modern *International Standard Version*, we understand the magic that is lost when plain English syntax is used:

> Peter said, 'I don't have any silver or gold, but I'll give you what I do have ...'

The transposition of the normal word order of English (subject–verb–complement: 'I | don't have | silver and gold') forcefully expresses the speaker's lack of material possessions ('silver and gold', itself a synecdoche for 'money').

The next example is from Keats's 'On First Looking into Chapman's Homer':

> Much have I travell'd in the realms of gold,
> And many goodly states and kingdoms seen

Regular English syntax would require Keats to say: 'I have travelled much in the realms of gold, and seen many goodly states and kingdoms'. However, Keats chooses to use hyperbaton. The adverb 'much' is transposed to the beginning of the sentence, the subject ('I') is inserted within two fragments of the verb ('have travell'd'), and, in the coordinate clause, the verb 'seen' is placed after the complement ('many goodly states and kingdoms').

Such inversion is a common feature of **poetic diction** (page 157). Longinus in his treatise *On the Sublime* (c. first century CE) held that the hyperbaton bore 'the very stamp and impress of vehement emotion' (an opinion that later critics have disagreed with). The

French psychoanalyst Jacques Lacan advises the reader to pay special attention to hyperbaton and other syntactical displacements in texts as they lead the reader to the speaker's unconscious.

Guided exercise

Explain the figure of speech in the lines given below.

1. *A slumber did my spirit seal*
   (Wordsworth, 'A Slumber Did My Spirit Seal')

2. But *the tongue no man can tame* (St James, The Epistle of James)

3. *Thrice is he armed* that hath his quarrel just
   (Shakespeare, *Henry VI, Part 2*)

4. *Sweet are the uses of adversity* (Shakespeare, *As You Like It*)

5. *Dull would he be of soul* who could pass by
   A sight so touching in its majesty
   (Wordsworth, 'Composed upon Westminster Bridge')

6. *Never saw I, never felt, a calm so deep!*
   (Wordsworth, 'Composed upon Westminster Bridge')

7. *Strange fits of passion have I known*
   (Wordsworth, 'Strange Fits of Passion Have I Known')

8. *From cocoon forth a butterfly*
   As lady from her door
   Emerged— (Dickinson, 'From Cocoon Forth a Butterfly')

9. *Just are the ways of God* (Milton, *Samson Agonistes*)

ANAPHORA OR EPANAPHORA

This figure consists in repeating a word or phrase at the beginning of successive clauses or sentences. Anaphora follows the logic of ritual recitations of words or sounds to reinforce an idea or to achieve an artistic or magical effect. Shakespeare's 'Sonnet 66', for example, repeats the conjunction 'and' at the beginning of ten of its fourteen lines. Martin Luther King Jr's most well-known speech uses anaphora through the refrain of the phrase 'I have a dream'. The next page lists two other examples.

When kind occasion prompts their warm desires,
When music softens, and when dancing fires
(Pope, *The Rape of the Lock*)

It was the best of times, it was the worst of times, it was
the age of wisdom, it was the age of foolishness, it was
the epoch of belief, it was the epoch of incredulity, it was
the season of Light, it was the season of Darkness, it was
the spring of hope, it was the winter of despair, we had
everything before us, we had nothing before us, we were
all going direct to Heaven, we were all going direct the
other way ... (Dickens, *A Tale of Two Cities*)

Guided exercise

Explain the figure of speech in the lines given below.

1. *Their's not to* make reply,
   Their's not to reason why,
   Their's but to do and die.
   (Tennyson, 'The Charge of the Light Brigade')

2. *Ring out* old shapes of foul disease;
   Ring out the narrowing lust of gold;
   Ring out the thousand wars of old,
   Ring in the thousand years of peace. (Tennyson, *In Memoriam*)

3. *Lost* wealth may be replaced by industry, *lost* knowledge by
   study, *lost* health by temperance or medicine, but *lost* time is
   gone forever. (Samuel Smiles, *Self-Help*)

EPISTROPHE OR EPIPHORA

This figure consists in the repetition of words or phrases at the
end of successive clauses, sentences or lines of verse for the sake of
emphasis or greater energy.

Wit is dangerous, eloquence is dangerous, a talent for
observation is dangerous, everything is dangerous that has
efficacy and vigour for its characteristics.
(Sydney Smith, 'Wit and Humour')

The sages are wrong, the great thinkers are wrong, scientists
are wrong, philosophers are wrong.

EIGHT

Figures based on Sound

ALLITERATION, CONSONANCE AND ASSONANCE

These three figures describe phonological recurrence, and are important elements in English versification from the days of Old English poetry.

The word 'alliteration' is derived from the Latin *littera*, meaning 'letter'. **Alliteration** is the repetition of initial consonant sounds in the stressed syllables of successive or nearly successive words.

Before English came to be influenced by Latin and French, it did not have many rhyming words. Poetry hinged upon the repetition of similar sounds in stressed syllables in a line of verse. Look at the following passage from *Beowulf*, the Old English epic:

> swefan æfter symble; sorge ne cuðon,
> wonsceaft wera. Wiht unhælo,
> grim ond grædig, gearo sona wæs,
> reoc ond reþe, ond on ræste genam
> þritig þegna, þanon eft gewat ...

> Asleep after supper, to sorrow unknown
> And misery of men. That monster unholy
> Gruesome and greedy, grabbed the opportunity;
> Ruthless, remorseless, from rest he seized
> Thirty thanes; and thence he hurried ...

The above lines do not have a rhyme scheme, but make use of repeated consonant sounds in the stressed syllables of key words. (For a detailed discussion on identifying **syllables** and **stress**, see pages 151–153.)

Even after the days of alliterative verse were over, alliteration remained a powerful element in English poetry. In 'Ode to a Nightingale', Keats describes a beaker of wine in the following words:

> With beaded bubbles winking at the brim

The stressed syllables are underlined. Note the repeating consonant sounds in the beginning of certain stressed syllables. The alliterating 'b' sound creates an impression of fullness and contentment.

In the following extract from Coleridge's 'The Rime of the Ancient Mariner', we observe alliterating 'b', 'f', and 's' sounds. (The stressed syllables are underlined. Most of the words are monosyllabic.)

> The fair breeze blew, the white foam flew,
> The furrow followed free;
> We were the first that ever burst
> Into that silent sea.

Consonance (sometimes called alliterative effect) is the repetition of consonant sounds in neighbouring words. Alliteration is a specific type of consonance in which the repeated consonant sounds appear at the *beginning* of stressed syllables. Consonance is a more general term which refers to the repetition of consonant sounds *anywhere* within words or within a verse passage.

In the following lines from Pope's *The Rape of the Lock*, consonant sounds are repeated not only in the stressed syllables (underlined) but also in the unstressed ones:

> Where wigs with wigs, with sword-knots sword-knots
>   strive,
> Beaux banish beaux, and coaches coaches drive.

Consonance is also seen in the following line from Coleridge's 'Frost at Midnight':

> ... that solitude, which suits / Abstruser musings

A related term, **assonance**, is the repetition of identical or similar vowel sounds in neighbouring words. Look at this example of assonance in the same line from Coleridge:

> ... that solitude, which suits / Abstruser musings

Like alliteration and consonance, assonance is used to create a musical effect. In the hands of skilful poets, assonance can even help develop a particular mood.

Here are some more examples of assonance.

> Thou still unravished bride of quietness,
> Thou foster child of silence and slow time
> (Keats, 'Ode on a Grecian Urn')

Repetition of the / ɪ / sound (st*i*ll, unrav*i*shed), and the /aɪ/ sound (br*i*de, qu*i*etness, ch*i*ld, s*i*lence, t*i*me)

That d*o*lphin-t*o*rn, that g*o*ng-t*o*rmented sea.
(Yeats, 'Byzantium')
Repetition of the /ɒ/ sound (d*o*lphin, g*o*ng), and the /ɔ:/ sound (t*o*rn, t*o*rmented)

Br*ea*k, br*ea*k, br*ea*k,
On thy c*o*ld gr*ey* st*o*nes, **O** Sea!
(Tennyson, 'Break, Break, Break')
Repetition of the /eɪ/ sound (br*ea*k, gr*ey*), and the /əʊ/ sound (c*o*ld, st*o*nes, **O**)

With regard to alliteration, consonance and assonance, it is important to keep in mind that we are talking about matching *sounds*, not letters. Remember that the English language does not have one-to-one correspondence between its alphabet and its sounds.

Guided exercise

Explain the figure of speech in the lines given below. Alliteration is marked in bold, consonance indicated through italics, and assonance is underlined.

1. His **fl**ashing eyes, his **fl**oating hair! (Coleridge, 'Kubla Khan')
   Remember: alliteration is the repetition of consonant sounds at the *beginning* of stressed syllables.

2. **P**uffs, **p**owders, **p**atches, **b**ibles, **b**illet-doux.
   (Pope, *The Rape of the Lock*)

3. I wie*l*d the f*l*ai*l* of the *l*ashing h<u>ai</u>*l* (Shelley, 'The Cloud')
   Remember: consonance is the repetition of consonant sounds *anywhere* in the line.

4. From *c*our*ts*, *c*amp*s*, to *c*ottage*s* it *s*tray*s*
   (Goldsmith, 'The Traveller')

5. <u>A</u>n <u>Au</u>st*r*ian a*r*m<u>y</u>, <u>a</u>wfull<u>y</u> <u>a</u>*rr*ay*e*d,
   *B*oldl<u>y</u> *b*y *b*atte*r*y *b*esiege*d* *B*elg*r*a<u>de</u>.
   (Watts, 'The Siege of Belgrade')
   Note the following with regard to the above lines—
   • There are three prominent instances of consonance here: the 'r', 'b' and 'd' sounds.

- There are four instances of assonance, of which the first two are seen in the first line. Although the words begin with the same vowel ('a'), each word begins with a different vowel *sound*. The initial sounds of 'Austrian' and 'awfully' (/ɒ/ and /ɔ:/, respectively), while not the same, are similar enough to be in assonance. In a like manner, the initial sounds of 'an', 'army' and 'arrayed' (/ə/, /ɑ:/ and /ə/, respectively) may be counted as an example of assonance because of the similarity between /ə/ and /ɑ:/.
- The third instance of assonance is seen in the final sound of 'army', 'awfully', 'boldly' and 'battery'. The letter 'y' may be a consonant in English, but the sound it represents in these words is a vowel sound, /i/. Hence, this is assonance, not consonance.
- The final instance of assonance is seen in the rhyming words 'arrayed' and 'Belgrade'. The underlined letters make the same /eɪ/ sound.
- If you are confused, simply pronounce the words (correctly) out loud, slowly and clearly—you will hear the sounds that match.

6. Alone, alone, all, all alone,
   Alone on a wide wide sea!
   (Coleridge, 'The Rime of the Ancient Mariner')
   Once again, note the many different instances of assonance in these two lines—
   - /ə/ sound in 'alone' and in 'a'
   - /ɔ:/ sound in 'all'
   - /əʊ/ sound in 'alone'
   - /aɪ/ sound in 'wide'
   There are also three instances of consonance and one instance of alliteration: spot them!

7. Nor cast one longing, lingering look behind
   (Gray, 'Elegy Written in a Country Churchyard')

8. The fair breeze blew, the white foam flew,
   The furrow followed free
   (Coleridge, 'The Rime of the Ancient Mariner')

9. Begot by butchers, but by bishops bred,
   How high his Highness holds his haughty head.
   Are these sounds examples of alliteration or consonance?

10. *S*light is the *s*ubject, but not *s*o the praise
    (Pope, *The Rape of the Lock*)

11. And thu*s* in whi*s*pers *s*aid, or *s*eem'd to *s*ay
    (Pope, *The Rape of the Lock*)

12. *S*ome *s*ecret truths, from learne*d* pri*d*e con*c*eal'*d*
    (Pope, *The Rape of the Lock*)
    Note that the italicised letter 'c' in the word 'concealed' has an
    's' sound, while the letter 's' in the word 'truths' has a 'z' sound.

13. Cool'*d* a long age in the *d*eep-*d*elvè*d* earth
    (Keats, 'Ode to a Nightingale')

PUN OR PARONOMASIA

A pun is a humorous play on words. In rhetoric, the word is an
umbrella term for several kinds of wordplay, such as paronomasia
(using words that sound alike but differ in meaning) and
antanaclasis (using a word or a phrase in different senses). Puns
usually involve *homophones* (words which sound alike, but have
different meanings and/or spellings) or *homographs* (words having
identical spelling but different meanings). The similar sounding or
looking words call forth two different senses and evoke laughter.
Let us consider a popular joke:

> A Frenchman jumped from the Eiffel tower, but the police
> did not arrest him because he was in Seine.

The Eiffel Tower in Paris is situated by the river Seine. 'In Seine' is
a homophone of 'insane'. The man jumped from the tower because
he was out of his mind (that is, insane) and landed in the river
(that is, in Seine). A pun like this one is a cerebral game: one of
the two homophones remains absent—the intelligent listener finds
it out and is amused. Another example of a homophonic pun is
the old slogan of Morrisons, the British supermarket chain—'More
reasons to shop at Morrisons'—with its playful use of the similar
sounds of 'more reasons' and 'Morrisons'.

The next example is a pun which employs homographs.

> He is a scientist, but his knowledge on sound is not sound.

Here, the first 'sound' (noun) means the science of audio signals,
and the next 'sound' (adjective) means deep or thorough. The joke

is understood when the meanings of the two homographs are clear. Here is another example that uses homographs:

> The conductor minds the train and a teacher trains the mind.

The meaning becomes clear once the listener considers the different meanings of the pair of homographs.

mind → verb → to attend to, to be in charge of
mind → noun → the seat of reason
train → verb → to instruct, to teach
train → noun → railway carriages

That is, the conductor is in charge of the railway carriage whereas the teacher instructs our rational faculty.

Shakespeare's plays abound in puns (referred to as 'quibbles' in his time). The playwright's fondness for wordplay made Samuel Johnson complain, 'A quibble is to Shakespeare, what luminous vapours are to the traveller; He follows it at all adventures; it is sure to lead him out of his way, and sure to engulf him in the mire. It has ... power over his mind, and its fascinations are irresistible.'

In *Twelfth Night*, Shakespeare plays with the homophones 'hart' (a stag, an adult male deer) and 'heart' (this second homophone is absent in the text). See how Shakespeare creates an extended metaphor by blending the pun with mythological associations.

CURIO: Will you go hunt, my lord?
ORSINO: What, Curio?
CURIO: The hart.
ORSINO: Why, so I do, the noblest that I have:
　　　　O, when mine eyes did see Olivia first,
　　　　Methought she purged the air of pestilence!
　　　　That instant was I turn'd into a hart;
　　　　And my desires, like fell and cruel hounds,
　　　　E'er since pursue me.

Curio asks if the Duke wishes to go stag-hunting ('hunt ... The hart'). Orsino replies that he is hunting his heart presently—'so I do [hunt], the noblest that I have [his heart being the noblest hart he has]'. He refers to the mythological story of Diana, the moon goddess, and Actaeon, the shepherd (see also **allusion**, page 42). Diana punished Actaeon by turning him into a stag (hart): the shepherd's own dogs hunted him down. Similarly, after seeing Lady Olivia, Orsino's 'heart' turned into a 'hart' and is being hunted by his own desires.

A famous example of a homophonic pun from *Hamlet* follows:

> KING: But now, my cousin Hamlet, and my son— ...
>   How is it that the clouds still hang on you?
> HAMLET: Not so, my lord; I am too much i' the sun.

Hamlet plays on the words 'sun' and 'son', which sound identical. Outwardly he declares that he is in the luminous presence (in the sun) of his uncle, the new king; so, there are no 'clouds' about him. However, Hamlet means to say that Claudius has called him 'son' too often.

Mercutio's famous dying statement in *Romeo and Juliet* uses a homographic pun:

> Ask for me tomorrow, and you shall find me a grave man.

Mercutio plays on the word 'grave', which can mean both 'sombre' and 'dead' (in the grave).

Guided exercise

Explain the figure of speech in the lines given below.

1. If a woman loses her husband, she pines for a *second*.

    Second = a short time; or a second husband

2. They went and *told* the sexton, and
    The sexton *toll'd* the bell.
    (Thomas Hood, 'Faithless Sally Brown')

    Told = expressed in words; tolled = rang a bell

3. It is no *mean* happiness ... to be seated in the *mean*.
    (Shakespeare, *The Merchant of Venice*)

    Mean = small/insignificant; or a middle position

4. Let me give *light*, but let me not be *light*.
    (Shakespeare, *The Merchant of Venice*)
    Light = illumination/guidance; or unchaste

5. Of Man's first disobedience, and the *fruit*
    Of that forbidden tree, whose mortal taste

Brought death into the world, and all our woe
(Milton, *Paradise Lost*)

Fruit = sweet, edible product of a tree; or result/consequence of
Man's disobedience

6. So is the *will* of a living daughter curbed by the *will* of a dead
father. (Shakespeare, *The Merchant of Venice*)

Will = desire/wish; or a legal document declaring a person's
wishes regarding the disposal of their property when they die

7. The tallest building in town is the library—it has thousands of
stories.

Story = a piece of fiction; storey = the level of a building

ONOMATOPOEIA

Onomatopoeia is the use of words that phonetically imitate a
natural or mechanical sound, and thereby convey meaning through
sound effects.

Hark, hark!
Bow-wow
The watch-dogs bark!
Bow-wow
Hark, hark! I hear
The strain of strutting chanticleer
Cry cock-a-diddle-dow! (Shakespeare, *The Tempest*)

Keats's line from 'Ode to a Nightingale' uses onomatopoeia to
describe a natural scene:

The murmurous haunt of flies on summer eves.

The 'm' and 's' sounds of 'murmurous' and 'summer,' and the 'z'
sounds at the end of 'flies' and 'eves' try to imitate and re-create
the immediacy of experience: the rustle of leaves and the buzzing
of flies. A close imitation of natural sounds can be found in the
following extract from Tennyson's 'The Brook':

I chatter over stony ways,
In little sharps and trebles,
I bubble into eddying bays,
I babble on the pebbles.

'Chatter', 'bubble' and 'babble' are examples of onomatopoeia as they signify the noise made by the moving water on different surfaces. Malcolm Peet and David Robinson point out that it is rare for words to be 'meaningful in themselves', and therefore onomatopoeia may be seen as a 'fortunate by-product of meaning' (*Leading Questions*).

Guided exercise

Explain the figure of speech in the lines given below.

1. And gathering swallows *twitter* in the skies.
   (Keats, 'To Autumn')

2. How they *tinkle, tinkle, tinkle,*
   In the icy air of night! (Poe, 'The Bells')

3. The ice *cracked* and *growled,* and *roared* and *howled*
   (Coleridge, 'The Rime of the Ancient Mariner')

   (See also **polysyndeton**, page 117.)

4. I heard the water *lapping* on the crag
   (Tennyson, *Morte D' Arthur*)

5. Only the monstrous anger of the guns,
   Only the *stuttering* rifles' rapid *rattle*
   Can *patter* out their hasty orisons.
   (Owen, 'Anthem for Doomed Youth')

6. Dry *clash'd* his harness, in the icy caves
   And barren chasms, and all to left and right
   The bare black cliff *clang'd* round him ...
   (Tennyson, *Morte d'Arthur*)

   Also mark the alliteration in the above lines.

NINE

Miscellaneous Figures

TAUTOLOGY

'Tautology', derived from the Greek *tautos* ('the same') and *logos* ('word' or 'idea'), refers to the repetition of an idea in different words; for example:

> He was quite exhausted and worn-out.
>
> They arrived one after another, in succession.
>
> The big giant was afraid of the tiny little insect.

Such repetition is usually regarded as a shortcoming in good writing since it is often the result of inattention on the part of the writer ('the enemy was surrounded on all sides').

However, as a rhetorical device, the use of multiple words or phrases that are similar in sense can convey emphasis or strong emotion; as in this example from Shakespeare's *The Taming of the Shrew*:

> O vile, intolerable, not to be endured!

Guided exercise

Explain the figure of speech in the lines given below.

1. He is an *impartial and neutral* judge.

2. Please deposit your *bag and baggage* at the counter.

3. We *rejoiced* at the *happy* sight.

    Note the **transferred epithet** (page 41) in 'happy sight'.

4. The boy is *hale and hearty*.

5. Freedom is our *first and foremost* objective.

PLEONASM

Pleonasm is a rhetorical term for excess of meaning. Derived from the Greek *pleon* ('too much'), pleonasm consists in the use of unnecessary words to express a single idea. Usually an impediment to concise writing, such repetitions can also indicate strong emphasis on an idea. Take a look at the examples below.

I saw it with my own eyes. (One sees with one's *own* eyes. However, this is not necessarily 'faulty' writing, because this pleonastic expression emphasises the immediacy of the speaker's experience.)

He eyed me with a look of contempt.

She had exclusive monopoly of the whole trade. (Monopoly means *exclusive* control.)

The boy has dishonestly stolen the book. (One can never steal *honestly*.)

At this moment in time (A moment is a particular point *in time*.)

He wept tears of joy.

An ancient handwritten manuscript (A manuscript is, by definition, *handwritten*.)

A free gift (Gifts are always *free*. However, advertisements often use this pleonasm to attract customers.)

Tautology and pleonasm

Tautology and pleonasm are both types of redundancy. A slight distinction may be made between the two—

| Tautology | *re-states something* using a different word/phrase with a similar meaning |
| Pleonasm | *uses more words than is required* to say something |

| Tautology | She was speeding too fast. |
| Pleonasm | Her rate of speed was high. |

'Speeding' means she was going 'too fast'. The same idea is reiterated. In the next sentence, the word 'rate' is superfluous, because 'speed' means the '*rate* of doing something'.

| Tautology | She looked at it and saw it. |
| Pleonasm | She saw it with her eyes. |

The first sentence is tautological because 'saw it' is a repetition of 'looked at it'. The second is pleonastic because 'she saw it' *implies* that she used 'her eyes'.

The practical difference between these two terms is usually blurry, and, with most everyday expressions, often boils down to splitting hairs.

Guided exercise

Explain the figure of speech in the lines given below.

1. The vote was *completely unanimous*.

   Unanimous = *complete* agreement

2. It was his *usual custom* to have breakfast at six in the morning.

   A custom is always *usual* or habitual.

3. The long-range missile can hit its *intended target* precisely.

   A target is never *unintended*.

4. Never disclose your *PIN number* to anyone.

   PIN = personal identification *number*

5. Picasso's style was *completely unique*.

   Unique = unequalled. Something can never be 'almost unique' or 'half-unique': there are no degrees of uniqueness.

PROLEPSIS

Prolepsis is an anachronistic representation of a future situation or action as already existing or accomplished. Here is a famous example from Keats's 'Isabella':

> So the two brothers and their murdered man
> Rode past fair Florence.

A 'murdered man' can never ride with his murderers. In this proleptic statement, we have a foreshadowing, an apprehension of the act of killing. This adds a dramatic touch to the lines.

Note also, these lines from Pope's *Pastorals*:

> Sing, then, and Damon shall attend the strain,
> While yon slow oxen turn the furrow'd plain.

The act of furrowing is anachronistically represented as already accomplished.

The following example from Scott's 'The Lady of the Lake' employs a series of prolepses to create a sense of regret over future wars:

> To know those spears our foes should dread
> For me in kindred gore are red:
> To know, in fruitless brawl begun,
> For me, that mother wails her son,
> For me, that widow's mate expires,
> For me, that orphans weep their sires,
> That patriots mourn insulted laws,
> And curse the Douglas for the cause.

In oratory, prolepsis meant the anticipation and answering of possible objections before they could be raised. (This device was also referred to as 'procatalepsis'.) In Chapter 4, we saw how **prosopopoeia** (page 71) is used to pre-emptively refute possible objections to one's argument. Prolepsis usually involves prosopopoeia; that is, prolepsis often *makes use of* prosopopoeia (a pretended dialogue) in order to counter objections before they are raised.

PARALEIPSIS

Paraleipsis is a figure of speech by which a writer or a speaker focuses attention on a subject by pretending to neglect it. It is sometimes spelt 'paralipsis', and is also known as 'apophasis'. Here are some examples:

> I will not say one word about his charity, his sincerity, or the nobility of his soul.

> For my part, I do not wish to say anything disagreeable about my incompetent and unqualified opponent.

It has the effect of highlighting the very thing that the speaker is pretending to dismiss or ignore. Mark Antony's funeral oration in Shakespeare's *Julius Caesar* contains perhaps the most famous example of paraleipsis in literature. He begins by saying 'I come to bury Caesar, not to praise him' and goes on to do just that. Later in the speech, he talks about Caesar's will:

Let but the commons hear this testament—
Which, pardon me, I do not mean to read—
And they would go and kiss dead Caesar's wounds
...
Have patience, gentle friends. I must not read it.
It is not meet you know how Caesar loved you.
You are not wood, you are not stones, but men.
And, being men, bearing the will of Caesar,
It will inflame you, it will make you mad.
'Tis good you know not that you are his heirs.
For, if you should—Oh, what would come of it!

Guided exercise

Explain the figure of speech in the lines given below.

1. The music, the service at the feast,
    The noble gifts for the great and small,
    The rich adornment of Theseus's palace, ...
    All these things I do not mention now.
    (Chaucer, *The Canterbury Tales*)

    The narrator does indeed mention a list of remarkable things.

2. *I will not even mention the fact that* you betrayed us ...
    (Cicero, *Catiline Orations*)

3. *I shall ignore the fact that* Learning is youth's finest ornament,
    the strong support of the prime of life, and the consolation of
    old age. (Milton, *Prolusions*)

CATACHRESIS

This figure consists in the wrong use of a word in a sense different
from but similar to its own. According to Pope, the masters of
catachresis will say:

> Mow the beard,
> Shave the grass,
> Pin the plank,
> Nail my sleeve. ('Peri Bathous')

Catachresis usually employs mixed metaphors. In Shakespeare's
The Tempest, a character says of another: 'His complexion is perfect

'gallows', meaning that his appearance ('complexion') is that of a criminal (someone destined for the 'gallows', that is, for death by hanging).

ORNAMENTAL EPITHET

This figure consists in the use of an adjective merely for the sake of beauty of expression, beyond which the adjective has no particular significance; for example:

O listen, listen, ladies gay! (Scott, 'Rosabelle')

APOSIOPESIS

Aposiopesis is 'rhetorical reticence', a break in the narrative, usually in moments of emotion. Derived from the Greek word for 'becoming silent', this figure consists of suddenly breaking off in the middle of what is written or said, and leaving the sentence incomplete for the sake of greater effect.

Here is an example from Shakespeare's *The Tempest*. When the king of Naples and his companions fall into a magical slumber, the villainous Antonio tries to persuade the king's brother Sebastian to murder the king. Antonio begins by thinking aloud about what they could do with such an opportunity, but stops dramatically to provoke Sebastian's curiosity.

They fell together all, as by consent.
They dropped, as by a thunderstroke. What might,
Worthy Sebastian, O, what might—? No more.—

In *King Lear*, the protagonist is so upset that his anger chokes his words.

I will have such revenges on you both,
That all the world shall— I will do such things,—
What they are, yet I know not: but they shall be
The terrors of the earth.

Guided exercise

Explain the figure of speech in the lines given below.

1. He catches her in his arms. The *fire surrounds them while—I cannot go on—* (Steele, *The Tatler* No. 94)

   Powerful emotion hinders the flow of narrative as Steele describes the death of a pair of lovers.

2. Must I remember? Why, she would hang on him
   As if increase of appetite had grown
   By what it fed on: and yet, *within a month—*
   Let me not think on't—Frailty, thy name is woman!
   A little month, or ere those shoes were old
   With which she follow'd my poor father's body,
   Like Niobe, all tears: Why she, *even she—*
   O, God! a beast, that wants discourse of reason
   Would have mourn'd longer—married with my uncle
   (Shakespeare, *Hamlet*)

3. Bear with me;
   My heart is in the coffin there with Caesar,
   And *I must pause till it come back to me.*
   (Shakespeare, *Julius Caesar*)

TEN

Exercises

Name and explain the figures of speech in the following lines.

1. The Lord is my rock, my fortress, and my deliverer

2. Time flies, death urges, knells call, heaven invites, hell threatens.

3. Come away, come away, death,
   And in sad cypress let me be laid;
   Fly away, fly away breath;
   I am slain by a fair cruel maid.

4. Life's but a walking shadow, a poor player

5. Love rules the court, camp, the grove,
   And men below, and saints above;
   For love is heaven and, heaven is love.

6. O grave, where is thy victory?

7. He was clad in steel.

8. It was the cradle and the grave of my military reputation.

9. The curfew tolls the knell of parting day

10. The ploughman homeward plods his weary way

11. Our birth is but a sleep and a forgetting

12. Sleep the sleep that knows not breaking

13. I pass, like night, from land to land

14. ... lowliness is young ambition's ladder

15. After life's fitful fever, he sleeps well.

16. Belinda smiled, and all the world was gay.

17. A small leak will sink a great ship.

18. Where palsy shakes a few, sad, last grey hairs,
    Where youth grows pale, and spectre-thin, and dies

19. We live in deeds, not in years.

20. England! with all thy faults I love thee still.

21. He was not the master but the slave of his speech.

22. ... women hate a debt as men a gift.

23. Beware the fury of a patient man.

24. O for a draught of vintage, that hath been
    Cooled a long age in the deep-delvèd earth,
    Tasting of Flora and the country-green
    Dance, and Provençal song, and sun-burnt mirth.

25. The busiest man has the amplest leisures.

26. If you prick us, do we not bleed?

27. And all Arabia breathes from yonder box.

28. They always talk who never think.

29. What though the field be lost?

30. The king is dead; long live the king.

31. He who has never hoped can never despair.

32. When husbands or when lap-dogs breathe their last

33. Stone walls do not a prison make

34. Tomorrow, and tomorrow, and tomorrow
    Creeps in this petty pace from day to day
    To the last syllable of recorded time;
    And all our yesterdays have lighted fools
    The way to dusty death.

35. He is not the brightest man in the world.

36. Sweet are the uses of adversity

37. The proper study of mankind is man.

38. O fearful meditation! Where, alack,
    Shall Time's best jewel from Time's chest lie hid?

39. A little noiseless noise among the leaves

40. ... 'twas a pleasing fear

41. His power was nil, his authority enormous.

42. He was a thief, a plunderer, an assassin.

43. Alone, alone, all, all alone, / Alone on a wide, wide sea!

44. They also serve who only stand and wait.

45. You blocks, you stones, you worse than senseless things!

46. Obliged by hunger and request of friends

47. Light gains make a heavy purse.

48. ... men are April when they woo, December when they wed

49. Private vices are public virtues.

50. O for a beaker full of warm South

51. She was reading Browning.

52. It amused the king not a little.

53. The kettle boils.

54. Give every man thy ear, but few thy voice.

55. She was playing to the gallery.

56. He keeps a good cellar.

57. They shift the moving toyshop of their heart

58. The operation was successful, though the patient died.

59. They are basking in the sun.

60. Grey hairs should be respected.

61. ... swiftly flies / The feathered death

62. Their furrow oft the stubborn glebe has broke

63. Sceptre and Crown / Must tumble down

64. A smooth tongue wins favour easily.

65. I have no roof to take shelter under.

66. ... wake the purple year

67. Silver and gold have I none.

68. After life's fitful fever he sleeps well.

69. The nineteenth autumn has come upon me

70. I am out of humanity's reach.

71. A career should be open to talent.

72. Youth is full of pleasure, age is full of care

73. He is a walking lie.

74. Thou still unravished bride of quietness

75. He allowed the father to be overruled by the judge, and declared his own son guilty.

76. She won the hearts of the people.

77. Man shall not live by bread alone

78. Thy word is a lamp to my feet.

79. He is a poor creature.

80. [Life] is a tale / Told by an idiot, full of sound and fury, / Signifying nothing.

81. He was killed in action.

82. Vessels large may venture more, / But little boats should keep near shore.

83. Hope is brightest when it dawns from fears.

84. Rome, thou hast lost the breed of noble bloods!

85. Her canvas drew praise.

86. She died laughing.

87. I do not consult physicians, for I hope to die without them.

88. His feet were bound in irons.

89. Some soldiers, I know, are afraid of death.

90. ... drowsy tinklings lull the distant folds

91. Some pious drops the closing eye requires

92. The reports of my death are greatly exaggerated.

93. Where lay the mighty bones of ancient men

94. And Niagara stuns with thundering sound.

95. Tyranny is dead!

96. He is the Newton of this century!

97. ... great pines groan aghast

98. ... Melancholy marked him for her own.

99. Where brooding Darkness spreads his jealous wings

100. ... Joy, whose hand is ever at his lips / Bidding adieu

101. Venice, the eldest Child of Liberty.

102. Fair laughs the morn

103. Sweet Auburn, loveliest village of the plain

104. England, with all thy faults, I love thee still

105. O Death, where is thy sting?

106. Roll on, thou deep and dark blue Ocean, roll!

107. Hail, holy light! Offspring of heaven first-born!

108. Mischief, thou art afoot!

109. I am tired to death!

110. Drink to me only with thine eyes

111. The house-roofs seemed to heave and sway

112. I loved a love once, fairest among women

113. ... no tongue / Their beauty might declare

114. The very deep did rot, O Christ!

115. A very fine friend you were to forsake me in my trouble.

116. She is proud of her wardrobe.

117. God made him and therefore let him pass for a man.

118. Sleep the sleep that knows not breaking

119. A favourite has no friend.

120. This is no common speech.

121. He drank the fatal cup.

122. He is no dullard.

123. With his usual punctuality he came after the train had gone.

124. It requires some knowledge to understand this.

125. The plumed members of the winged tribe gathered together.

126. Full fathom five thy father lies

127. To gossip is a fault; to libel, a crime; to slander, a sin.

128. Puffs, powders, patches, bibles, billet-doux.

129. The moan of doves in immemorial elms

130. What's hit is history; what's missed is mystery.

131. If he do bleed, / I'll gild the faces of the grooms withal

132. Am I not free to do as I choose?

133. Art lies in concealing art.

134. O, what a fall was there, my countrymen!

135. Out of evil cometh good

136. Smooth runs the water where the brook is deep

137. Round many western islands have I been

138. What a piece of work is a man!

139. He rushed into the field, and, foremost fighting, fell.

140. My days among the Dead are past

141. For he on honey-dew hath fed

142. Ruin seize thee, ruthless king!

143. A slumber did my spirit seal

144. Man is a hater of truth, a lover of fiction.

145. ... all its aching joys are now no more

146. ... this world! / ...'Tis an unweeded garden

147. Out of suffering comes the serious mind

148. The petty done, the undone vast

149. ... may you stand long, and long stand the terror of tyrants

150. I am become a name

151. And singing still dost soar, and soaring ever singest.

152. Perfume and flowers fell in showers

153. An hundred years should go to praise / Thine eyes

154. Beauty cannot keep her lustrous eyes

155. The feast and noon grew high

156. I come to bury Caesar, not to praise him.

157. The moment flitted and the vessel passed.

158. He was relieved of the post.

159. His looks drew attention and audience.

160. Down to the pool and narrow wharf he went

161. Smelling of musk and of insolence

162. Excess of ceremony shows want of breeding.

163. We'll hear him, we'll follow him, we'll die with him.

164. She has a fluent tongue.

165. She dropped a tear and her pocket handkerchief.

166. O sylvan Wye! thou wanderer through the woods

167. It was a false lie.

168. Better to reign in hell, than serve in heaven.

169. And Niagara stuns with thundering sound

170. Heard melodies are sweet, but those unheard / Are sweeter

171. Theirs be the music, the colour, the glory, the gold

172. Death lays his icy hand on kings

173. Envy and calumny, and hate and pain

174. I see no reason to recount the lunches, dinners, horses, and presents that attended his arrival.

175. It isn't very serious. I have this tiny little tumour on the brain.

PROSODY

Introduction

Prosody (derived from the Greek word *prosōidía*, meaning 'a song sung to music') is the study of the technical elements of poetry. In order to appreciate poetry, apart from understanding the ideas present in it, we also need to learn the mechanisms employed in a particular composition, because it is these mechanisms which enable a piece of verse to breathe and dance and command our attention.

This introductory section has two parts:

1. a brief survey of various kinds of poetry
2. an introduction to a few technical terms related to prosody

Familiarity with these types and terms (and others which we will learn in subsequent chapters) will help us analyse lines of verse.

KINDS OF POETRY
Descriptive poetry

This kind of poetry describes, among other things, cities, places, countries, the seasons of the year, and scenes of historical interest. It expresses the thoughts and feelings connected with its subject. Goldsmith's 'The Traveller' and 'The Deserted Village' are instances of descriptive poetry.

Narrative poetry

In this form of poetry, the narration of events is the primary aim, and description is secondary. Epics, romances, legends and ballads come under this class of poetry.

Epic or heroic poetry

It is a long poetical composition narrating, in great detail, the achievements of a legendary or national hero, or a grand action of national or cosmic importance, in a dignified style. Milton's

Paradise Lost, Homer's *Iliad* and *Odyssey*, and Keats's *Endymion* and *Hyperion* are examples of such poems.

Romance, legend or tale

Compared to epics, these are shorter kinds of narrative poetry, dealing with incidents of life, real or imaginary, past or present. Coleridge's 'The Rime of the Ancient Mariner' and Tennyson's *Idylls of the King* are good examples.

Pastoral

This kind of poetry deals with the life of shepherds, herdsmen and husbandmen. These poems are usually in the form of a dialogue or a monologue. The pastoral is an old form of poetry and is now seldom attempted by poets. Milton's 'Lycidas' and Spenser's *The Shepheardes Calender* are instances of the pastoral form.

Ballad

A ballad is a poem in short stanzas narrating a popular story. The language and metre are often crude; the passion and the situation depicted, usually simple. This form of verse originated from dancing songs. Ballads express broad human emotions related to war, love, crime, superstition or death. Cowper's 'John Gilpin' and Wordsworth's *Lyrical Ballads* are instances.

Lay

This is another type of lyrical narrative poetry that is intended to be sung by minstrels. It deals with semi-historical romantic stories. Scott's 'The Lay of the Last Minstrel' is an example.

Lyric

It is a short subjective piece of poetry, written in rapid and irregular metre. This form of poetry originated in ancient Greece, and was composed to be sung or recited in accompaniment with the lyre. Milton's 'L'Allegro' and 'Il Penseroso', and Shelley's 'The Cloud' are some instances of lyric poems. The elegy, the ode, and the sonnet are different types of lyric poetry.

Elegy

An elegy is a lamentation for the dead. Milton's 'Lycidas', Shelley's 'Adonaïs' and Gray's 'Elegy Written in a Country Churchyard' are instances of elegies.

Ode

An ode is a lyrical piece of poetry, usually taking the form of an address. It is sublime in its subject, and exalted in tone, feeling and style. Keats's 'Ode to a Nightingale' and 'To Autumn', and Shelley's 'To a Skylark' are fine examples of the ode.

Sonnet

The sonnet is a short subjective poem dealing with one thought or emotion, and written in fourteen iambic pentameter lines with a specific arrangement of rhymes. Shakespeare's sonnet sequence, Spenser's *Amoretti* poems, and Milton's 'On His Blindness' are examples of sonnets.

Didactic poetry

Didactic poetry is written to convey some moral, religious or philosophical lesson. Pope's *Essay on Man* and *Moral Essays* are instances of didactic poetry.

Satire

It is a kind of didactic poetry which points out the faults of individuals or communities, and may be written in either a serious or a humorous vein. Dryden's *Absalom and Achitophel* and Butler's *Hudibras* are good examples.

Villanelle

A villanelle is a poem of nineteen lines arranged in a very specific structure and having a rigid rhyme scheme. Although its origins lie in French pastoral poetry, the villanelle has been used for a wide range of themes in English poetry. Dylan Thomas's 'Do Not Go Gentle into that Good Night' is an excellent example of this poetic form.

Free verse

Free verse is a kind of poetry that does not use a consistent metrical or rhyming pattern. Rhythm in free verse poetry matches the cadences of natural speech, and structure varies from poem to poem depending upon subject, themes and imagery. Free verse generally allows the poet more freedom than metrical compositions. Popularised by the American poet Walt Whitman's *Leaves of Grass*, the majority of poetry in English published since the twentieth century has been free verse. However, experiments in free verse may be seen in English literature as far back as the King James Bible.

TERMS USED IN PROSODY

Syllable

A syllable is a unit of spoken language uttered in one effort. It may be an entire word, or just a part of a word.

A syllable, as a unit of pronunciation, contains only one vowel sound. Note that we are talking about vowel *sounds*, not vowel *letters*. English has only five vowel letters (*a, e, i, o, u*); but there are 20 vowel sounds in modern English (Received Pronunciation).

Monosyllabic words:	go, inn, debt, break
Disyllabic words:	expert (ex–pert), absent (ab–sent), slowly (slow–ly)
Trisyllabic words:	capital (ca–pi–tal), engineer (en–gi–neer), beautiful (beau–ti–ful)

Remember that diphthongs count as a single vowel sound.

Accent or stress

In prosody, the term 'accent' denotes a vocal stress, emphasis or effort laid on certain syllables of words, which marks these syllables off from the other syllables by greater distinctness in pronunciation.

Say the following words aloud, and note which syllable in each word sounds more prominent:

monarchy	mo–nar–chy	mo–nar–chy	accent/stress on the first syllable
religion	re–li–gion	re–li–gion	accent/stress on the second syllable
engineer	en–gi–neer	en–gi–neer	accent/stress on the third syllable

The stressed syllable is indicated by placing an accent mark (ˊ) over the vowels of the stressed syllable. Similarly, unstressed syllables of a word are indicated by placing a breve symbol (˘) over the vowels of the unstressed syllables. For example:

ˊ ˘ ˘	˘ˊ ˘	˘ ˘ ˊ
monarchy	religion	engineer

Rules governing accent in English

Knowing which syllable of a word to stress is important—not merely for prosody, but for correct English pronunciation in general. The following guidelines will be helpful. However, always remember that there are exceptions to every rule, and that these rules are sometimes broken in versification.

1. Stress the first syllable of most two-syllable nouns and adjectives.

   For example: éxpèrt, sátìre, ábsènt, bárrèn

2. Stress the last syllable of most two-syllable verbs and prepositions.

   For example: commènd, dèný, amòng, betwèen

   Note that the same word may be stressed differently depending on whether it is being used as a noun or a verb.

   For example: óbjèct (noun), òbjéct (verb),

   éxpòrt (noun), èxpórt (verb)

3. Stress the syllable immediately before the following suffixes: *–able*, *–ery*, *–ia*, *–ial*, *–ian*, *–ible*, *–ic*, *–ient*, *–ion*, *–ious*, *–ish*, and *–sis*.

   For example: dúrable, commèndable, mèdia, geográphic, mýstèry, mystérìous

4. Stress the ante-penultimate (third-last) syllable of words that end in the following suffixes: *–al*, *–cy*, *–gy*, *–phy*, and *–ty*.

   For example: geográphical, geógraphy, nationálity

Words of more than three syllables may seem to have more than one stressed syllable; for example: everlasting, nationality, radiology. However, English words always have only one syllable that is prominently stressed, and it is more important to know where this primary stress falls (everlasting, nationality, radiology). The secondary stress is always a significantly weaker stress.

When analysing verse lines, you will need to mark the stressed and unstressed syllables with accent (∕) and breve (◡) marks respectively. Keep the following in mind when doing so.

1. Always place these marks over the vowels, and never over the consonants.

2. The accent usually falls on the root syllable.

   $\acute{\ }\ \smile\ \smile\ \acute{\ }$
   dark–ness, en–slave

3. Prefixes are *not* accented.

   $\smile\ \acute{\ }\ \smile\ \acute{\ }$
   un–wise, be–ware

4. Suffixes are *not* accented.

   $\acute{\ }\ \smile\ \acute{\ }\ \smile\ \smile$
   slow–ly, love–li–ness

5. In words of more than three syllables, the secondary stress may be marked if it helps identify the rhythm of a line.

   $\acute{\ }\ \smile\ \acute{\ }\ \smile$
   ev–er–last–ing

6. Monosyllabic articles, pronouns, prepositions and conjunctions (for example: *a, an, and, but, for, from, in, it, of, on, since, the, with,* and so on) are generally *not* accented.

Rhythm

Rhythm is a regular pattern of movement or sound. Your heart beats in a particular rhythm. This rhythm can be fast (when you are excited) or slow (when you are relaxed), but the repetition of sounds is always evident. Other examples of rhythm may be heard in the marching of soldiers or in the galloping of a horse.

In both oral and written literature, rhythm can be created through the arrangement of long and short sounds, or stressed and unstressed syllables. The periodical recurrence of pauses and accents produces a harmonious effect. Rhythm is a quality of both prose and poetry. The difference between prose and poetry is that the latter makes use of versification—that is, words, phrases and lines are carefully and deliberately arranged and organised to produce specific rhythms. In other words, verse is measured composition.

Rhyme

It is the recurrence of similar sounds (especially in the closing syllables) in lines of verse. Look at the following lines:

> And are those follies going?
> And is my proud heart growing
> Too cold or wise
> For brilliant eyes (Moore, 'The Time I've Lost in Wooing')

Up Jack *got*, and home did *trot*
As fast as he could caper;
To old Dame *Dob*, who patched his *nob*
With vinegar and brown paper. ('Jack and Jill')

How *small*, of *all* that human hearts en<u>dure</u>,
That part which *laws* or kings can *cause* or <u>cure</u>. (Goldsmith,
'The Traveller')

A **masculine rhyme** is one in which a single stressed syllable bears
the rhyme. For example, *wise–eyes*. A **feminine rhyme** is one in
which the final unstressed syllable bears the rhyme. For example,
go*ing*–grow*ing*, cap*er*–pap*er*. An **end rhyme** occurs when the
rhyming words fall at the end of lines. For example, go*ing*–grow*ing*,
wise–eyes, cap*er*–pap*er*, en*dure*–*cure*. An **internal rhyme** occurs
when the rhyming words fall within a line. For example, *got–trot*,
Dob–nob, *small–all*, *laws–cause*.

Rhyme is to be distinguished from rhythm. Both feature
repetition or recurrence; but while rhyme is the repetition of
vowel sounds, rhythm is the repetition of a recognisable pattern
of stresses.

See page 173 for a short note on **rhyme scheme**.

Pause

When reading lines of verse, we pause at the end of a sentence, or at
the end of a clause, or when the sense demands it. The punctuation
in poetry is often a good indicator of when to pause. When a pause
naturally coincides with the end of a line of verse, such a line is
called an **end-stopped line**. Some verse lines force the reader to
carry on without a pause onto the next line. This feature is known
as **enjambment**, and such lines are called **run-on lines**. A pause
may also occur within a line of verse; such a pause is termed a
caesura (plural: caesurae). A caesura is indicated using double
vertical lines (‖). Caesurae may be found towards the beginning, in
the middle, or towards the end of a line, and are accordingly called
initial, medial or terminal caesura, respectively.

Read aloud the following lines from Shakespeare's *Hamlet*, and
note the pauses.

To be, or not to be, ‖ that is the question: (1)
Whether 'tis nobler in the mind to suffer (2)

The slings and arrows of outrageous fortune,   (3)
Or to take Arms against a Sea of troubles,   (4)
And by opposing end them: ‖ to die, to sleep ...   (5)

Lines 1 and 5 contain prominent examples of caesurae. Line 1 is end-stopped, whereas Line 2 is a run-on line (the sense of the line carries on without a pause into Line 3).

Measure or foot

A 'foot' is a combination of unaccented and accented syllables. In each English foot, there is one accented syllable and one or two unaccented syllables. For example:

| water | | she mourns | | like the wolf |

A foot is marked off from other feet using a vertical line (|). A poetic foot is the basic unit used to measure the length of a line of poetry. The following verse line has five feet.

That time | of year | thou may'st | in me | behold

The standard feet in English verse are as follows.

1. **Trochee** (adjective: trochaic): stressed syllable, followed by unstressed syllable
   Once u- | pon a | midnight | dreary

2. **Iamb** (or, **iambus**; adjective: iambic): unstressed syllable, followed by stressed syllable
   The hand | that held | my wrist

3. **Dactyl** (adjective: dactylic): stressed syllable, followed by two unstressed syllables
   Charge for the | guns! he said

4. **Anapaest** (adjective: anapaestic): two unstressed syllables, followed by stressed syllable
   The Assy- | rian came down | like the wolf | on the fold

5. **Amphibrach** (adjective: amphibrachic): stressed syllable between two unstressed syllables
   There once was | a girl from | Nantucket

Two other types of feet often appear in English verse as variants from the standard feet.

6. **Spondee** (adjective: spondaic): two stressed syllables

7. **Pyrrhic** (adjective: pyrrhic): two unstressed syllables

To a | green thought | in a | green shade

The first and third feet are pyrrhic, while the second and fourth feet are spondaic.

Trochee, iamb, spondee and pyrrhic are *disyllabic feet*. Dactyl, anapaest (spelled 'anapest' in American English) and amphibrach are *trisyllabic feet*.

Verse lines are named according to the number of feet they contain.

A line containing one foot is called **monometer**. Similarly, lines with—

two feet	**dimeter**
three feet	**trimeter**
four feet	**tetrameter**
five feet	**pentameter**
six feet	**hexameter**
seven feet	**heptameter**

... and so on. The number of feet in English verse usually varies from two to seven.

Metre

Metre (spelled 'meter' in American English) is the rhythmic structure of lines of verse. While rhythm may be found in both prose and poetry, metre is what usually sets them apart. A metrical line (that is, a line of verse) is one in which the rhythm has been manipulated and arranged into regular units of specific length in order to create a musical effect.

There are different methods of analysing poetic metre. This book will introduce you to the most common method, which identifies metre by the character and number of feet in lines of verse. You will learn how to do this in subsequent chapters.

Scansion

Scansion is the process of identifying the metre of a poem. When we 'scan' a verse passage, we examine its rhythm by marking the stressed and unstressed syllables in it, and then point out the nature and number of feet in it. You will learn how to scan a poem in the next chapter.

POETIC DICTION

Poetic diction is the peculiarity in the form and use of words and their construction in lines of poetry. Poetry sounds and looks (on the printed page) different from speech and written prose. This difference is because of the way it uses language, and this special usage of language is referred to as poetic diction.

Poetic diction is the result of the following.

1. Use of archaic and Latinate words
   For example, *thou* for 'you'; *vale* for 'valley'; *haply* for 'perhaps'; *azure* for 'blue'

2. Lengthening or shortening of words
   For example, *begirt* for 'girt'; *even* for 'evening'; *am'rous* for 'amorous' (see **elision**, page 200)

3. Omission of parts of speech
   For example, *Lives there who loves his pain?* instead of 'Lives there *a man* who loves his pain?'

4. Violation of grammar
   For example, 'The ploughman *homeward plods* his weary way': the adverb is placed before the verb

5. Circumlocution (that is, roundabout wording)
   For example, *twice five miles* instead of 'ten miles'

6. Use of figures of speech
   Poetry tends to be richer in rhetorical devices (particularly simile, metaphor, metonymy, synecdoche, personification, alliteration and apostrophe) than prose.

ONE

Metrical Feet, and How They 'Walk'

Metre is the organised rhythm of a poem, and a characteristic feature of traditional poetry. In this chapter, you will learn how to recognise the metrical pattern of a verse passage. You will also be introduced to many of the poetic metres found in English poetry.

HOW METRES ARE NAMED

The metre of a verse passage is named after (1) the *dominant foot* of that passage and (2) the *number of feet* in a line of verse from the passage.

See, for example, the following lines from Shelley's 'To a Skylark'.

High-er | still and | high-er

From the | earth thou | spring-est

As you have learnt in the Introduction, the stressed syllables are indicated with an accent mark (ˊ), while the unstressed syllables are indicated using a breve (˘) symbol.

Each foot of the lines above contains a stressed syllable followed by an unstressed syllable. You have learnt in the Introduction (page 155) that such a foot is called a 'trochee'. Since all the feet in these two lines are trochees as well, we can say that the *dominant foot* of this passage is trochaic.

Now count the *number of feet* in each line. There are three feet in each line. You have learnt in the Introduction (page 156) that such a line is called a trimeter.

To identify the metre of a verse passage, we name the dominant foot and the number of feet. Thus, we can say that the metre of these lines from 'To a Skylark' is trochaic trimeter.

Here are two more examples, both from Byron.

> She walks | in beau- | ty, like | the night
>
> Of cloud- | less climes | and star- | ry skies ('She Walks in Beauty')

Dominant foot: iamb; number of feet per line: four; therefore, metre: iambic tetrameter

> The Assy- | rian came down | like the wolf | on the fold,
>
> And his co- | horts were gleam- | ing in pur- | ple and gold
> ('The Destruction of Sennacherib')

Dominant foot: anapaest; number of feet per line: four; therefore, metre: anapaestic tetrameter

How to Scan Verse

You have learnt what 'metre' is. But how does one determine what metre a verse passage is set in? The process of measuring the rhythm of a poem and analysing its metre is known as *scansion*.

Scansion is one of the tools of prosody. This section will take you step-by-step through the process of scanning a verse passage. Let us once again use Shelley's lines from 'To a Skylark' as an example of a verse passage to be scanned. The purpose of this exercise is to identify the metre of these lines, and to indicate if there are any variations in its rhythm.

Step 1

Read the given lines aloud a few times—first at a normal tempo, and then slow down your pace of reading so that the rhythm of the lines may become apparent.

Higher still and higher	(1)
From the earth thou springest .	(2)
Like a cloud of fire;	(3)
The blue deep thou wingest,	(4)
And singing still dost soar, and soaring ever singest.	(5)

Step 2

Break up the words (except monosyllabic ones) of each line into their component syllables using hyphens; for example: higher = high-er, singest = sing-est.

English is notorious for its lack of correspondence between spelling and pronunciation. When in doubt, say the word aloud, slowly, till the syllables become clear to you. For example, the word 'fire' (Line 3) has two syllables: faɪ-ə.

Step 3

Next, indicate the stressed syllables, placing the mark over the vowel of the accented syllable.

> Hígh-er stíll and hígh-er
>
> Fróm the éarth thou spríng-est
>
> Líke a clóud of fí-re;
>
> The blúe déep thou wíng-est,
>
> And síng-ing stíll dost sóar, and sóar-ing év-er síng-est.

This is an important step: a misplaced accent may lead to incorrect scansion of a verse passage. Knowing the correct pronunciation of a word is very helpful in identifying its stressed syllables. (Most dictionaries indicate the accented syllables of a word; when in doubt, reach for a good dictionary.)

Remember that an accent usually falls on the root syllable of a word, and not on a prefix or a suffix. Remember also that an accent usually falls on a more important word or a more important part of a word. An accent does not usually fall on an article, pronoun, preposition, conjunction or interjection. For more helpful hints, see pages 152–153 for the 'Rules governing accent in English'. Never try to force an accent on a syllable in order to make it fit a discernible pattern: accents should be placed where they occur naturally in everyday speech, or as per the sense of a line.

Step 4

Now, indicate the unstressed syllables, placing the mark over the vowel of the unaccented syllable.

> Hígh-ĕr stíll ănd hígh-ĕr
>
> Fróm thĕ éarth thŏu spríng-ĕst

´ ˘ ´ ˘ ´ ˘
Like a cloud of fi-re;

˘ ´ ´ ˘ ´ ˘
The blue deep thou wing-est,

˘ ´ ˘ ´ ˘ ´ ˘ ´ ˘ ´ ˘ ´ ˘
And sing-ing still dost soar, and soar-ing ev-er sing-est.

Step 5

Count the number of syllables and the number of accents in each line.

If the number of syllables in a line is double or about double the number of accents in the line, then the dominant foot of that line is likely to be disyllabic. If the syllables are treble or close to treble the number of accents, then the dominant foot of the line is likely to be trisyllabic.

Line 1	syllables: 6	accents: 3	disyllabic foot	
Line 2	syllables: 6	accents: 3	disyllabic foot	...and so on
Line 5	syllables: 13	accents: 6	disyllabic foot	

Step 6

Mark the feet, and then count the number of feet in each line.

If Step 5 indicated a disyllabic foot, draw a vertical line (|) after each group of two syllables, to mark each foot of a line of verse; if trisyllabic, draw the vertical line after each group of three syllables.

´ ˘ ´ ˘ ´ ˘
High-er | still and | high-er   (3 feet)

´ ˘ ´ ˘ ´ ˘
From the | earth thou | spring-est   (3 feet)

´ ˘ ´ ˘ ´ ˘
Like a | cloud of | fi-re;   (3 feet)

˘ ´ ´ ˘ ´ ˘
The blue | deep thou | wing-est,   (3 feet)

˘ ´ ˘ ´ ˘ ´ ˘ ´ ˘ ´ ˘ ´ ˘
And sing- | ing still | dost soar, | and soar- | ing ev- | er sing- | est.
                                                                (6 feet)

Do not hesitate to split up a word when marking feet. Feet are marked based on accents (sound), and not based on writing. See, for example, the way Line 5 has been divided.

Note that a single unaccented syllable does not count as a foot. Therefore, the last line has six feet (not seven).

Step 7

Identify the dominant foot.

In a disyllabic metre, when the first syllable of a foot is accented, the metre is trochaic; when the second syllable is accented, it is iambic. A foot with both syllables accented is spondaic; and one with both syllables unaccented is pyrrhic.

A metre with trisyllabic feet in which only the first syllable is accented is dactylic; when only the last syllable is accented, it is anapaestic; and when only the middle one is accented, it is amphibrachic.

In the example passage, the recurring rhythmic pattern of the first four lines is the trochee, which is the dominant foot of this stanza. The last line, however, is iambic.

Step 8

You now know the dominant foot, as well as the number of feet in each line. Name the metre of the given poem.

Shelley's 'To a Skylark', for example, is written primarily in trochaic trimeter.

Step 9

The final step in scansion is to identify and comment on variations in the metre of a verse passage.

All the lines of a piece of poetry may not be of the same metre. Even within a single verse line, it is common to find variations that violate the metrical pattern of the line. Poets may introduce variations in metre in order to dispel the monotony caused by a uniform rhythm, or to create musical effects, or to call attention to certain parts of the poem. Variations in metre are usually of three kinds:

- *substitution* (or 'inversion') of the dominant foot with another foot
- *addition* of an accented or unaccented syllable at the beginning or at the end of a line
- *omission* of an unaccented syllable at the beginning of a line

Regarding variations, keep the following in mind.

- An iambic line may have trochees, spondees, pyrrhics or anapaests as variations, but rarely dactyls.
- A trochaic line may have iambs and dactyls as variations.

- An anapaestic line may have only iambs as variations.
- A dactylic line may have only trochees as a variation.
- Two-syllable English words have one accented syllable. However, in trisyllabic measures, words pronounced quickly, such as *very*, *many*, *any*, and so on, are sometimes not accented.
- Lines at the end of which unaccented syllables are dropped are called 'catalectic'. Lines from the beginning of which unaccented syllables are dropped are called 'acephalous'. Lines ending in an unaccented syllable not required by the metre are called 'hypermetrical'. You will learn more about these terms in the next chapter.

Scansion is not complete until you have identified the metre of the poem as well as the variations in the rhythm. To return to our example, we can conclude our analysis of Shelley's verse by stating:

> The first four lines are written in trochaic trimeter. The first foot of the fourth line is iambic. The final line is written in iambic hexameter, and is hypermetrical.

METRES IN ENGLISH VERSE

Now that we know how to determine the metre of a poem, let us look at some examples of poetic metres found in English verse. (Some of the verse lines below contain variations from the stated metre. Can you spot these variations?)

Trochaic metre

The trochaic metre consists of disyllabic feet in which the first syllable is accented and the second syllable is unaccented. Due to its stress pattern, it is regarded as a 'falling metre'. As it has two syllables per foot, it is also known as a 'duple metre'. A trochaic metre is usually suited to gay and lively subjects because of its brisk gait and dancing movement. It is also used in devotional poetry.

Trochaic monometer

Turn-ing

Burn-ing

Chang-ing

Rang-ing

Trochaic dimeter

> Rích thĕ | tréa-sŭre
>
> Swéet thĕ | pléa-sŭre

Trochaic trimeter

> Whén hĕ | wás bŭt | thír-tў
>
> Jóhn wăs | léan ănd | dír-tў

Trochaic tetrameter

> Máy, thŏu | mónth ŏf | ró-sў | beáu-tў
>
> Mónth whĕn | pléa-sŭre | ís ă | dú-tў

Iambic metre

The iambic metre is another example of a duple metre. It consists of disyllabic feet in which the first syllable is unaccented and the second syllable is accented. This stress pattern makes it a 'rising metre'. The smooth, stately and graceful iambic metre is the chief metre in English poetry. It is generally employed in narrative and descriptive poetry. Nearly all English sonnets are in iambic pentameter.

Iambic monometer

> Ĭ knów
>
> Thĕ wáy,
>
> Yĕt gó
>
> Ă-stráy.

Iambic dimeter

> Mў Bóok | ănd Heárt
>
> Mŭst né- | vĕr párt.

My on- | ly books

Were wo- | men's looks.

The light, | that lies

In wo- | man's eyes

Iambic trimeter

Why do | ye fall | so fast?

Your date | is not | so past.

For us | the win- | ters rain;

For us | the sum- | mers shine;

Spring swells | for us | the grain,

And au- | tumn bleeds | the vine.

Iambic tetrameter (or Romantic metre)

If such | there breathe, | go, mark | him well

For him | no min- | strel's rap- | tures swell

And then | my heart | with plea- | sure fills

And dan- | ces with | the daf- | fo-dils.

Iambic pentameter (or heroic verse)

Be-side | yon stragg- | ling fence | that skirts | the way

With blos- | somed furze | un-pro- | fi-tab- | ly gay.

Unrhymed iambic pentameter lines are known as **blank verse**. Also known as 'heroic verse' because of its use in epic poetry, blank verse is the predominant metre of English dramatic verse, as well as of long philosophical or narrative poems. Some of the masterpieces of English literature, including Shakespeare's plays and Milton's *Paradise Lost*, have been written in this measure. Blank verse poems are not divided into stanzas of fixed length.

Note this example of blank verse from Shakespeare's *Romeo and Juliet*.

> But soft! | What light | through yon- | der win- | dow breaks?
>
> It is | the east, | and Ju- | liet is | the sun.
>
> A-rise, | fair sun, | and kill | the en- | vious moon,
>
> Who is | al-rea- | dy sick | and pale | with grief,
>
> That thou, | her maid, | art far | more fair | than she.

It is important to distinguish blank verse from free verse (see page 150). The unrhymed lines of blank verse have a definite metrical pattern—iambic pentameter—and therefore a regular arrangement of rhythm. Free verse, on the other hand, does *not* have a consistent metrical pattern: its rhythm is irregular and varies from poem to poem. Blank verse often tends to be more musical than free verse.

Iambic hexameter (or alexandrine verse)

> To draw | men as | they ought | to be, | not as | they are
>
> The dew | was fal- | ling fast, | the stars | be-gan | to blink.

A line in iambic hexameter is called an **alexandrine**. (The name is derived from the use of a similar metre in a medieval French poem on Alexander the Great.) In English verse, it is rare for an entire poem to be in composed in alexandrines. Instead, alexandrines are more commonly used as variations among lines written in other (usually iambic) metres. On page 159, Line 5 of the extract from Shelley's 'To a Skylark' is an alexandrine.

Iambic heptameter

> And swee- | ter far | is death | than life, | to me | that long | to go

Dactylic metre

This falling metre consists of trisyllabic feet in which the accent falls on the first syllable. It is a common measure, and is generally found mixed up with other metres. As it has three syllables per foot, it is also known as a 'triple metre'.

Dactylic dimeter

 Come a-way, | come a-way

 Can-non to | right of them,

 Can-non to | left of them,

 Touch her not | scorn ful-ly

 Think of her | mourn-ful-ly

Dactylic trimeter

 Long may the | tree, in his | ban-ner that | glances,

 Flou-rish, the | shel-ter and | grace of our | line!

 Know ye the | land where the | cy-press and | myrtle

The dactylic trimeter is seldom found pure, without additional accented syllables or variations.

Anapaestic metre

Anapaestic metre is a rising triple metre. The accent in its trisyllabic feet falls on the final syllable, while the first two syllables remain unaccented.

Anapaestic dimeter

 With his ham- | mer of wind,

 And his gra- | vel of frost

Anapaestic trimeter

I am mon- | arch of all | I sur-vey

The de-sire | of the moth | for the star ...

The de-vo- | tion to some- | thing a-far

Anapaestic tetrameter

And his low | head and crest, | just one sharp | ear bent back

You may break | you may shat- | ter the vase, | if you will

Like a child | from the womb, | like a ghost | from the tomb

Amphibrachic metre

It has trisyllabic feet in which the middle syllable is accented, while the first and the third syllables remaining unaccented.

Amphibrachic dimeter

The warm sun | is fail-ing

The bleak wind | is wail-ing

The bare boughs | are sigh-ing

Amphibrachic trimeter

Di-vi-ding | and gli-ding | and sli-ding

Amphibrachic tetrameter

There came to | the beach a | poor ex-ile | of Er-in

The dew on | his thin robe | was hea-vy | and chill

Special Cases: Differently Formed Feet

Poetry is not mechanically produced. Though there are rules regarding versification, there will always be deviations which add to the beauty of the pattern. In this chapter, we will discuss some such variations that we often come across in verse passages.

The spondaic foot

A spondee is a disyllabic foot in which both the syllables are accented. As the English language makes use of a combination of accented and unaccented syllables to create sense and rhythm, a poem in which every single syllable is accented would sound very strange. For this reason, there is no spondaic metre in English, and the spondee is an irregular foot that appears as a variation in lines written in other metres. A spondee slows down the tempo of a metrical line.

The pyrrhic foot

The pyrrhic is a disyllabic foot in which both the syllables are unaccented. Since accented syllables are important in English, a poem written in pyrrhic feet would sound monotonous. The pyrrhic foot is therefore used only to vary the rhythm of a line, particularly by speeding up its tempo.

Ŏ mád- | nĕss! tŏ | thínk úse | ŏf stróng- | ĕst wínes

The second foot is pyrrhic, and the third foot is spondaic.

Ĭn thăt | sweét moód | whĕn pleá- | sănt thoúghts

The first foot is pyrrhic, and the second foot is spondaic.

The catalectic line

'Catalectic' is derived from a Greek word meaning 'stopping short'. It is a metrically incomplete line in which the last foot requires one or two unaccented syllables to make it complete. However, the incomplete foot is still counted as a foot (because of the presence of the accented syllable), and the line is called catalectic.

Life is | short and | time is | swift x

Ro-ses | fade and | sha-dows | shift x

The above lines are in catalectic trochaic tetrameter.

The acephalous line

This is a variation of the catalectic line. Acephalous means 'headless'. Lines from the beginning of which unaccented syllables are dropped are called acephalous. Just as in catalectic lines, the first incomplete foot is still counted as a foot.

x Weigh | the ves- | sel up

The above line is a 'headless' iambic trimeter or acephalous iambic trimeter.

A note on acephalous and catalectic lines

Both acephalous and catalectic lines are results of the dropping of unaccented syllables. In an acephalous line, the unaccented syllable is dropped at the beginning of the line. In a catalectic line, the unaccented syllable is dropped at the end.

It follows therefore that a trochaic line without the unaccented final syllable is the same as an iambic line without the initial syllable. See, for example, the following catalectic trochaic tetrameter lines from Auden.

Lay your | sleep-ing | head, my | love, x

Hu-man | on my | faith-less | arm x

Some feel justified in scanning trochaic catalectic verses as iambic acephalous, and vice versa.

x Lay | your sleep- | ing head, | my love,

x Hu- | man on | my faith- | less arm

Before naming a variant line as iambic or trochaic, check to see the metre of the poem as a whole.

Anacrusis

Anacrusis is a prefix of one or two unaccented syllables to a verse generally beginning with an accented syllable.

Blake's 'The Tyger' is in trochaic tetrameter catalectic for the most part, as demonstrated by the first of the two lines given below. But the next line contains an anacrusis: it begins with an unaccented syllable ('And') instead of the stressed syllable one expects from a trochaic metre.

When the | stars threw | down their | spears x

And | wa-ter'd | hea-ven | with their | tears x

The hypermetrical line

Verses ending in unaccented syllables not required by the metre are called hypermetrical. The last unaccented syllable is not counted as a foot.

On the | hope-less | fu-ture | pon-der- | ing

The above line is trochaic tetrameter hypermetrical.

With clouds | and sky | a-bout | thee ring- | ing

The above line is iambic tetrameter hypermetrical.

Sprung rhythm

All the metrical forms that you have read about so far have a fixed pattern of stresses and a fixed number of syllables in each line of verse. However, there are other types of versification as well. The nineteenth-century British poet Gerard Manley Hopkins coined the term 'sprung rhythm' for a metrical form that he believed best approximated the natural rhythms of English speech.

Sprung rhythm does not have a set stress pattern or any restriction on the total number of syllables in a line of verse. Instead, it has a fixed number of strong syllables per line, with a variable number of weak syllables. This allows the poet more freedom than the metres you are familiar with, while maintaining the constraints of metrical composition.

Look at the following example of sprung rhythm from Hopkins's sonnet 'No worst, there is none', and note the fixed number of stressed syllables per line. (The scansion for sprung rhythm follows slightly different rules from what you have learnt, with emphasis often falling on musical beat rather than on phonological accent.)

> O the mind, mind has mountains; cliffs of fall
>
> Frightful, sheer, no-man-fathomed. Hold them cheap
>
> May who ne'er hung there. Nor does long our small
>
> Durance deal with that steep or deep. Here! creep,
>
> Wretch, under a comfort serves in a whirlwind: all
>
> Life death does end and each day dies with sleep.

Although both blank verse and sprung rhythm attempt to imitate the cadences of spoken English, the former is more structured and follows an iambic rhythm while the latter has a looser rhythm. Sprung rhythm is also different from free verse in that it is a metrical composition—it has a fixed number of 'strong' syllables (free verse has no constraints on its rhythm, stresses, syllables, feet or rhymes).

Rhyme Schemes and Stanza Patterns

In the previous chapters, you were introduced to some of the elements of poetry. In addition to the terms you have already learnt, it would be helpful know the common rhyme schemes and stanza patterns found in English verse.

Rhyme scheme

Rhyme creates connections between lines of verse. The repetition of certain rhymes in regular patterns can enhance such connections. A rhyme scheme is the pattern of end rhymes found in a group of verse lines. Rhyme schemes are usually represented by lower case letters, with each letter representing a particular instance of end rhyme.

Notice the pattern of end rhymes in the opening lines of Wordsworth's poem 'I Wandered Lonely as a Cloud'.

I wandered lonely as a cloud	*a*
That floats on high o'er vales and hills,	*b*
When all at once I saw a crowd,	*a*
A host, of golden daffodils;	*b*
Beside the lake, beneath the *trees*,	*c*
Fluttering and dancing in the *breeze*.	*c*

The rhyme scheme of the above verse passage is *ababcc*. This scheme of rhymes is repeated throughout the poem.

Stanza

Verse lines within a poem often appear in fixed groups or sets called stanzas. The lines of a stanza often (but not always) have a specific number of feet arranged in a specific metre. Some stanzas have recognisable rhyme schemes, others do not. Stanzas usually function as units of sense within a poem.

A **couplet** is a pair of verse lines. A typical couplet consists of two rhyming lines of a similar length in the same metre. The grammatical sense of a couplet may be complete in itself, or the sense may run on to the next lines of the verse passage.

A **heroic couplet** is a pair of rhyming lines set in iambic pentameter. It is so called because of its use in English translations of heroic and epic poems by neoclassical writers. Such couplets are common in the heroic poems of Dryden and in the didactic poems of Pope.

> Achilles' wrath, to Greece the direful spring
> Of woes unnumber'd, heav'nly goddess, sing!
> (Pope's translation of *The Iliad*)

A **distich** is a closed couplet containing a pithy saying or an idea complete in itself.

> An idler is a watch that wants both hands;
> As useless when it goes as when it stands.
> (Cowper, 'Retirement')

A **tercet** is a three-line stanza. A tercet in which all three lines have the same end rhyme (that is, the rhyme scheme is *aaa*) is called a **triplet**. Tercets are the building blocks of the terza rima (see below) and the villanelle (see page 150). Unrhymed tercets are used to compose haikus.

A **quatrain** is a stanza of four verse lines. Quatrains have been employed in literature around the world, and have many possible rhyme schemes.

A five-line stanza is called a pentastich; a stanza of six lines, a hexastich; and so on.

Certain verse forms with specific combinations of stanzas, rhyme schemes and poetic measures have special names. These are detailed below.

Terza rima

The terza rima is a form of verse that consists of interlocked tercets. The three-line stanzas of the terza rima are linked using the following rhyme scheme: *aba bcb cdc ded*, and so on. In English poetry, the terza rima is usually set in iambic pentameter. Shelley's 'Ode to the West Wind' is an example of this verse form.

Ballad stanza

A ballad stanza is a quatrain consisting of alternating tetrameter and trimeter lines that rhyme either *xaxa* (the *x* stands for unrhymed lines) or *abab*. The name comes from its use in folk ballads. Coleridge uses this stanza form in 'The Rime of the Ancient Mariner'.

Elegiac stanza

It consists of an iambic pentameter quatrain rhyming *abab*. It is mainly used in elegies or plaintive poems. Also referred to as a 'heroic stanza', the term 'elegiac stanza' became popular after its use in Gray's 'Elegy Written in a Country Churchyard'.

Tennysonian stanza

It consists of an iambic tetrameter quatrain rhyming *abba*. Tennyson's *In Memoriam* has been written in this stanza form (hence its alternate name, the 'In Memoriam stanza').

Rhyme royal (or Chaucerian stanza)

Also spelt 'rime royal', this stanza form consists of seven lines, usually set in iambic pentameter, rhyming *ababbcc*. Its first English appearance was in the poetry of Geoffrey Chaucer. It was until recently believed that the name of this stanza form derived from its use by King James I of Scotland in his verse. Shakespeare's *Rape of Lucrece* is written in rhyme royal.

Ottava rima

The ottava rima is an eight-line stanza consisting usually of eleven syllables that rhyme *abababcc*. The ottava rima in English verse is often set in iambic pentameter, and has been used by Byron in *Don Juan*.

Spenserian stanza

This nine-line stanza form consists of eight iambic pentameter lines followed by a final iambic hexameter line (that is, an alexandrine), rhyming *ababbcbcc*. This stanza form was invented by Edmund Spenser for *The Faerie Queene*. Keats uses Spenserian stanzas in 'The Eve of St Agnes'.

As with any other technical feature in poetry, it is not enough to merely identify rhyme schemes and stanza patterns; you should try and understand how they *function* in a particular poem. Recognising such formal features and using appropriate terminology is the first step—the real task is to examine how these rhyme schemes are used in the poem and what effects they create.

Stanzas can be seen as obvious units of sense within a poem. For example, in a Petrarchan sonnet, the first eight lines (the 'octave') tend to form one unit of sense, and the last six lines (the 'sestet'), another. The octave usually presents a problem or describes a situation, while the sestet provides a response to the problem or situation (in the form of a personal reaction, an illustration, a proposed solution, and so on).

In the Shakespearean sonnet, the problem or situation is developed in three quatrains. Each quatrain dwells on one aspect of the issue. The sonnet ends with a rhyming couplet which briefly sums up the situation in an epigrammatic fashion or offers a punch line which ironically contrasts with the preceding discussion.

Rhyme schemes form units of sound within a poem, enhancing its musical qualities. Moreover, because rhyme schemes form audible connections between lines of verse, they too can suggest units of sense. The initial quatrains of Frost's 'Stopping by Woods on a Snowy Evening' have the following rhyme scheme: *aaba bbcb ccdc*. This gives the sense of stopping, and then carrying on, which is mirrored in the lines of the poem.

Apart from marking units of sense, rhyme schemes can suggest meanings on their own, too. The alternating *abab* pattern, for instance, suggests movement or playfulness, while the enclosed *abba* structure creates associations of something more static, stately and dignified. Tercets, especially with the terza rima rhyme scheme, also suggest movement and dynamism, while couplets tend to create a halt, giving the impression that something is finished or completed (this is clearly the function of the closing couplet of the English sonnet).

Thus we see that rhyme schemes and stanza patterns are not mere ornament in poetry. In addition to musicality, they can be used by skilful poets to add layers of meaning and depth to a poem.

FOUR

Guided Exercise: Scansion of Verse Passages

Art is not arithmetic. Scansion is not like doing a sum where the answer is the same for all. This, however, does not mean that in the realm of art, anarchy reigns supreme. It only means that there may be honest differences of opinion with regard to details in scansion. A slight difference in opinion will not spoil the value of scansion. But an accent must be rightly placed, for it is the soul of scansion. So far as the prevailing metre is concerned, there must be full agreement.

This chapter will show you several examples of scanned verse passages. Note how these lines have been scanned; this will serve as a guide when you are scanning verse on your own.

———

Ring out the grief that saps the mind
   For those that here we see no more;
   Ring out the feud of rich and poor,
Ring in redress to all mankind.   (Tennyson, 'In Memoriam')

Rĭng oút | thĕ grief | thăt sáps | thĕ mínd

   Fŏr thóse | thăt hére | wĕ sée | nŏ móre;

   Rĭng oút | thĕ feúd | ŏf rích | ănd poór,

Rĭng ín | rĕ-dréss | tŏ áll | măn-kínd.

The above lines are in iambic tetrameter. (Such a quatrain rhyming *abba* is referred to as a Tennysonian stanza.)

The curfew tolls the knell of parting day,
  The lowing herd wind slowly o'er the lea,
The ploughman homeward plods his weary way,
  And leaves the world to darkness and to me.

(Gray, 'Country Churchyard')

The cur- | few tolls | the knell | of par- | ting day,

  The low- | ing herd | wind slow- | ly o'er | the lea,

The plough- | man home- | ward plods | his wea- | ry way,

  And leaves | the world | to dark- | ness and | to me.

These lines are in iambic pentameter. (The given passage is an elegiac stanza: an iambic pentameter quatrain rhyming *abab*.)

Alone she cuts and binds the grain,
And sings a melancholy strain;
O listen! for the Vale profound
Is overflowing with the sound. (Wordsworth, 'The Solitary Reaper')

A-lone | she cuts | and binds | the grain,

And sings | a me- | lan-cho- | ly strain;

O lis- | ten! for | the Vale | pro-found

Is o- | ver-flow- | ing with | the sound.

The lines given above have been composed in iambic tetrameter.
  Take a look at the end rhymes in the lines above. Can you say what the rhyme scheme is?

He went like one that hath been stun'd,
And is of sense forlorn:
A sadder and a wiser man,
He rose the morrow morn.

(Coleridge, 'Rime of the Ancient Mariner')

Hĕ wént | lĭke óne | thăt háth | bĕen stúnn'd,

Ănd ís | ŏf sénse | fŏr-lórn:

Ă sád- | dĕr ánd | ă wĭ- | sĕr mán,

Hĕ róse | thĕ mór- | rŏw mórn.

In this stanza, the poet alternates lines of iambic tetrameter and iambic trimeter.

What is such a stanza form called? See page 175 for the answer.

————

When that the poor have cried, Caesar hath wept:
Ambition should he made of sterner stuff:
Yet Brutus says he was ambitious;
And Brutus is an honourable man.   (Shakespeare, *Julius Caesar*)

Whén thăt | thĕ póor | hăve críed, | Cáe-săr | hăth wépt:

Ăm-bí- | tiŏn shóuld | bĕ máde | ŏf stér- | nĕr stúff:

Yĕt Brú- | tŭs sáys | hĕ wás | ăm-bĭ- | tiŏus

Ănd Brú- | tŭs ís | ăn hó- | nŏu-rá- | blĕ mán.

The given lines are in iambic pentameter. The first line has two variations: its first and fourth feet are trochees. The third line is tetrametric and hypermetrical.

————

When I consider how my light is spent
Ere half my days, in this dark world and wide,
And that one Talent which is death to hide
Lodg'd with me useless, though my Soul more bent
To serve therewith my Maker, and present
My true account, lest He returning chide
(Milton, 'On His Blindness')

Whĕn Í | cŏn-sí- | dĕr hów | mў líght | ĭs spént

Ĕre hálf | mў dáys | ĭn thís | dărk wórld | ănd wíde,

And that | one Tal- | lent which | is death | to hide

Lodg'd with | me use- | less, though | my Soul | more bent

To serve | there-with | my Ma- | ker, and | pre-sent

My true | ac-count, | lest He | re-turn- | ing chide

The lines are written in iambic pentameter. The first foot of the fourth line is trochaic.

———

By the shores of Gitche Gumee,
By the shining Big-Sea-Water,
Stood the wigwam of Nokomis,
Daughter of the Moon, Nokomis.
Dark behind it rose the forest,
Rose the black and gloomy pine-trees,
Rose the firs with cones upon them;
Bright before it beat the water,
Beat the clear and sunny water,
Beat the shining Big-Sea-Water.
                    (Longfellow, 'Hiawatha's Childhood')

By the | shores of | Git-che | Gum-ee,

By the | shi-ning | Big-Sea- | Wa-ter,

Stood the | wig-wam | of No- | ko-mis,

Daugh-ter | of the | Moon, No- | ko-mis.

Dark be- | hind it | rose the | fo-rest,

Rose the | black and | gloo-my | pine-trees,

Rose the | firs with | cones u- | pon them;

Bright be- | fore it | beat the | wa-ter,

Beat the | clear and | sun-ny | wa-ter,

Beat the | shi-ning | Big-Sea- | Wa-ter.

Longfellow set these lines in trochaic tetrameter, with the following variations: the second, the sixth, and the tenth lines have a spondee as their third, fourth, and third feet respectively.

I listen'd, motionless and still;
And, as I mounted up the hill,
The music in my heart I bore,
Long after it was heard no more.

                      (Wordsworth, 'The Solitary Reaper')

Ĭ lís- | tĕn'd, mó- | tiŏn-léss | ănd stíll;

Ănd, ás | Ĭ moún- | tĕd úp | thĕ híll,

Thĕ mú- | sĭc ín | mў héart | Ĭ bóre,

Lóng áf- | tĕr ít | wăs héard | nŏ móre.

This passage is in iambic tetrameter. The final line begins with a spondee.

NOTE

The first foot of the final line goes against the iambic rhythm. 'Long' should be stressed as the vowel sound in the word is a long one, and the word itself is key to the sense of the line.

The rock shone bright, the kirk no less,
That stands above the rock:
The moonlight steep'd in silentness
The steady weathercock. (Coleridge, 'Rime of the Ancient Mariner')

Thĕ róck | shŏne bríght, | thĕ kírk | nŏ léss,

Thăt stánds | ă-bóve | thĕ róck:

Thĕ moón- | lĭght steép'd | ĭn sí- | lĕnt-néss

Thĕ steá- | dў weá- | thĕr-cóck.

The first and third lines of this ballad stanza are in iambic tetrameter, while the second and fourth lines are in iambic trimeter. The rhyme scheme is *abab*.

O judgement! thou art fled to brutish beasts,
And men have lost their reason. Bear with me;
My heart is in the coffin there with Caesar,
And I must pause till it come back to me.

(Shakespeare, Julius Caesar)

Ó judge- | ment! thou | art fléd | to brú- | tish béasts,

And men | have lóst | their réa- | son. Bear | with mé;

My heart | is in | the cóf- | fin there | with Cáe- | sar,

And I | must pause | till it | come back | to me.

The metre of this verse passage is iambic pentameter. The first line
begins with a spondee. The third line is hypermetrical.

___

Home they brought her warrior dead:
She nor swooned, nor uttered cry:
All her maidens watching said,
She must weep or she will die.

(Tennyson, 'Home They Brought Her Warrior Dead')

Home they | brought her | war-rior | dead:

She nor | swooned, nor | ut-tered | cry;

All her | mai-dens | watch-ing | said,

She must | weep or | she will | die.

The above lines are in trochaic tetrameter. The last foot of every
line is catalectic.

___

Far from the madding crowd's ignoble strife,
    Their sober wishes never learn'd to stray;
Along the cool sequester'd vale of life
    They kept the noiseless tenor of their way.

(Gray, 'Country Churchyard')

Far from | the mad- | ding crowd's | ig-no- | ble strife,

Their so- | ber wish- | es ne- | ver learn'd | to stray;

A-long | the cool | se-ques- | ter'd vale | of life

They kept | the noise- | less te- | nor of | their way.

The metre is iambic pentameter, with an initial trochaic inversion in the first line.

Judge, O you gods, how dearly Caesar loved him!
This was the most unkindest cut of all;
For when the noble Caesar saw him stab,
Ingratitude, more strong than traitors' arms,
Quite vanquishd him: then burst his mighty heart
(Shakespeare, Julius Caesar)

Judge, O | you gods, | how dear- | ly Cae- | sar loved | him!

This was | the most | un-kind- | est cut | of all;

For when | the no | ble Cae- | sar saw | him stab,

In-gra- | ti-tude, | more strong | than trai- | tors' arms,

Quite van- | quishd him: | then burst | his migh- | ty heart.

Shakespeare wrote these lines in iambic pentameter, with a few variations. The first line is hypermetrical. The first foot of the first line is a spondee. The first foot of the second line is a trochee.

It little profits that an idle king,
By this still hearth, among these barren crags,
Match'd with an aged wife, I mete and dole
Unequal laws unto a savage race,
That hoard, and sleep, and feed, and know not me.
(Tennyson, 'Ulysses')

Ĭt lĭt- | tlĕ pró- | fĭts thát | ăn í- | dlĕ kíng,

Bў thĭs | stíll heárth, | ă-móng | thĕse bár- | rĕn crágs,

Mátch'd wĭth | ăn á- | gĕd wífe, | Ĭ méte | ănd dóle

Ŭn-é- | quăl láws | ún-tŏ | ă sá- | văge ráce,

Thăt hóard, | ănd sléep, | ănd féed, | ănd knów | nŏt mé.

These lines are in iambic pentameter. The variations are as follows: (1) in the second line, the first foot is pyrrhic and the second foot is spondaic; (2) in the third line, the first foot is trochaic; (3) in the fourth line, the third foot is trochaic.

I cannot rest from travel: I will drink
Life to the lees: all times I have enjoy'd
Greatly, have suffer'd greatly, both with those
That loved me, and alone; on shore, and when
Thro' scudding drifts the rainy Hyades
Vext the dim sea: I am become a name;
For always roaming with a hungry heart   (Tennyson, 'Ulysses')

Ĭ cán- | nŏt rést | frŏm trá- | vĕl: Í | wĭll drínk

Lífe tŏ | thĕ leés: | áll tímes | Ĭ hăve | ĕn-jóy'd

Gréat-lў, | hăve súf- | fĕr'd gréat- | lў, bóth | wĭth thóse

Thăt lóved | mĕ, ánd | ă-lóne; | ŏn shóre | ănd whén

Thrŏ' scúd- | dĭng drífts | thĕ raí- | nў Hý- | ăd-és

Véxt thĕ | dĭm séa: | Ĭ ám | bĕ-cóme | ă náme:

Fŏr ál- | wăys róam- | ĭng wíth | ă húng- | rў heárt

The dominant metre is iambic pentameter, with a trochaic substitution in the first foot of the second, third, and sixth lines. The second line has a spondee in the third foot, followed by a pyrrhic in the next foot.

Note

The second line may also be scanned more simply—without the spondee and pyrrhic—as:

Life to | the lees: | all times | I have | en-joy'd

However, when scanning a verse passage, keep the meaning of the passage in mind as well. Poets often introduce variations in rhythm in order to draw attention to something. In the above line, 'all' is a key word, necessary with regard to the sense of the line (and with regard to the speaker's self image): Ulysses is somewhat proud of the fact that exciting adventures, and moments of great joy and great suffering, happened to him *all* the time (rather than occasionally, as in the life of an average person). Hence, the word 'all' is stressed, resulting in a forceful spondee ('all times'). Conversely, 'I have' plays only a functional role in that line, and there's no need for 'have' to bear an accent. The pyrrhic balances the effect of the spondee, allowing Tennyson to maintain the beat of the verse.

Let not Ambition mock their useful toil,
   Their homely joys, and destiny obscure;
Nor Grandeur hear with a disdainful smile
   The short and simple annals of the Poor.

(Gray, 'Country Churchyard')

Let not | Am-bi- | tion mock | their use- | ful toil,

   Their home- | ly joys, | and des- | ti-ny | obs-cure;

Nor Grand- | eur hear | with a | dis-dain- | ful smile

   The short | and sim- | ple an- | nals of | the Poor.

Gray's well-known lines are in iambic pentameter. There are a couple of variations in the third line: the spondee in the first foot is balanced by a pyrrhic in the third foot.

This is my son, mine own Telemachus,
To whom I leave the sceptre and the isle—
Well-loved of me, discerning to fulfil

This labour, by slow prudence to make mild
A rugged people, and thro' soft degrees
Subdue them to the useful and the good.
Most blameless is he, centred in the sphere
Of common duties, decent not to fail
In offices of tenderness, and pay
Meet adoration to my household gods,
When I am gone. He works his work, I mine.   (Tennyson, 'Ulysses')

This is | my son, | mine own | Te-le- | ma-chus,

To whom | I leave | the scep- | tre and | the isle—

Well-loved | of me, | dis-cern- | ing to | ful-fil

This la- | bour, by | slow pru- | dence to | make mild

A rug- | ged peo- | ple, and | thro' soft | de-grees

Sub-due | them to | the use- | ful and | the good.

Most blame- | less is | he, cen-| tred in | the sphere

Of com- | mon du- | ties, de- | cent not | to fail

In of- | fi- ces | of ten- | der- ness, | and pay

Meet a- | do-ra- | tion to | my house- | hold gods,

When I | am gone. | He works | his work, | I mine.

The above lines are in unrhymed iambic pentameter (that is, blank verse), with a few variations that make the verse approximate the turns of natural speech—(1) first line, first foot: trochee; (2) third line, first foot: spondee; (3) fourth line, second foot: pyrrhic; (4) fourth line, third foot: spondee; (5) fourth line, fourth foot: pyrrhic; (6) fourth line, fifth foot: spondee; (7) tenth line, first foot: trochee.

NOTE

Take a look at the fourth line:

This la- | bour, by | slow pru- | dence to | make mild

Tennyson was very fond of this spondee–pyrrhic combination. He uses the heavy spondees to *slow down* the pace of the line when talking about the difficult labour of civilising ('make mild') the 'rugged people' which will take time, patience and care ('slow prudence'). The vowel sounds are appropriately long ones. The pyrrhics in the line fall into place due to relative stress.

Hail to thee, blithe spirit!
Bird thou never wert,
That from heaven, or near it,
Pourest thy full heart
In profuse strains of unpremeditated art.   (Shelley, 'To a Skylark')

Hail to | thee, blithe | spir-it!

Bird thou | ne-ver | wert,

That from | heaven, or | near it,

Pour-est | thy full | heart,

In pro- | fuse strains | of un- | pre-me- | di-ta- | ted art.

The first four lines are in trochaic trimeter. The last line is an alexandrine, that is, iambic hexameter. There are a few variations. The first line contains a spondee in its second foot. The second and fourth lines are catalectic. There is a dactyl in the second foot of the third line.

Can you point out the rhyme scheme?

There, through the summer day,
Cool streams are laving;
There, while the tempests sway,
Scarce are boughs waving   (Scott, *Marmion*)

There, through the | sum-mer day,

Cool streams are | lav-ing;

There, while the | tem-pests sway,

Scarce are boughs | wav-ing

These lines are in dactylic dimeter. The second foot of both the second and the fourth lines is trochaic.

When I think of my own native land,
In a moment I seem to be there;
But, alas! recollection at hand
Soon hurries me back to despair.

(Cowper, 'The Solitude of Alexander Selkirk')

When I think | of my own | na-tive land,

In a mo- | ment I seem | to be there;

But, a-las! | re-col-lec- | tion at hand

Soon hur- | ries me back | to des-pair.

The given lines are in anapaestic trimeter. The first foot of the final line is iambic. The third line has a caesura at the end of the first foot.

Since brass, nor stone, nor earth, nor boundless sea,
But sad mortality oersways their power,
How with this rage shall beauty hold a plea,
Whose action is no stronger than a flower?

(Shakespeare, 'Sonnet 65')

Since brass, | nor stone, | nor earth, | nor bound- | less sea,

But sad | mor-ta- | li-ty | oer-sways | their pow- | er,

How with | this rage | shall beau- | ty hold | a plea,

Whose ac- | tion is | no strong- | er than | a flow- | er?

The verse is in iambic pentameter with minor variations. The second and the fourth lines are hypermetrical. The first foot of the third line is trochaic. The rhyme scheme is *abab*.

Now fades the glimmering landscape on the sight,
　And all the air a solemn stillness holds,
Save where the beetle wheels his droning flight,
　And drowsy tinklings lull the distant folds
(Gray, 'Country Churchyard')

Nŏw fádes |thĕ glím- |mĕr-ĭng lánd- |scăpe ón |thĕ síght,

　Ănd áll |thĕ áir |ă so- |lĕmn stíll- |nĕss hólds,

Sáve whĕre |thĕ bee- |tlĕ wheéls |hĭs drón- |ĭng flíght,

　Ănd drŏw- |sў tínk- |lĭngs lúll |thĕ dís- |tănt fólds

The metrical pattern of these lines is iambic pentameter, with an anapaestic variation in the third foot of the first line, and a trochaic inversion in the first foot of the third line.

Note

The third line breaks the iambic pattern momentarily by beginning with a trochee. 'Save' (meaning 'except') is a key word in this line because it marks a turn in the sense, and therefore needs to be stressed. (Conversely 'where' does not need to be stressed, since the location of the beetle/sheep is not important, but rather, the sound being made.)

Save that from yonder ivy-mantled tow'r
　The moping owl does to the moon complain
Of such, as wandering near her secret bow'r,
　Molest her ancient solitary reign.　(Gray, 'Country Churchyard')

Sáve thăt |frŏm yón- |dĕr í- |vў-mán- |tlĕd tów'r

　Thĕ mo- |pĭng ówl |doĕs tŏ |thĕ moón |cŏm-pláin

Ŏf súch, |ăs wánd'r- |ĭng neár |hĕr séc- |rĕt bów'r,

　Mŏ-lést |hĕr án- |cĭĕnt so- |lĭ-tă- |rў réign.

This passage is composed in iambic pentameter, with trochaic substitutions in the first foot of the first line and in the third foot of the second line. The rhyme scheme is *abab*.

The ice was here, the ice was there,
The ice was all around:
It crack'd and growl'd, and roar'd and howl'd,
Like noises in a swound!

(Coleridge, 'Rime of the Ancient Mariner')

Thĕ íce | wăs hére, | thĕ íce | wăs thére,

Thĕ íce | wăs áll | ă-róund:

Ĭt cráck'd | ănd grówl'd, | ănd róar'd | ănd hówl'd,

Lĭke nóis- | ĕs ín | ă swóund!

The metre of the given passage is iambic, with alternating tetrameter and trimeter lines.

Can storied urn or animated bust
   Back to its mansion call the fleeting breath?
Can Honour's voice provoke the silent dust,
   Or Flatt'ry soothe the dull cold ear of Death?

(Gray, 'Country Churchyard')

Căn stór- | ĭed úrn | ŏr ă- | nĭ-má- | tĕd búst

   Báck tŏ | ĭts mán- | sĭon cáll | thĕ fléet- | ĭng bréath?

Căn Hó- | nŏurs vóice | prŏ-vóke | thĕ sí- | lĕnt dúst,

   Ŏr Flátt'- | rў sóothe | thĕ dúll | cóld éar | ŏf Déath?

These lines are written in iambic pentameter. The first foot of the second line is trochaic, and the fourth foot of the fourth line is a spondee.

Full many a gem of purest ray serene,
   The dark unfathom'd caves of ocean bear:
Full many a flow'r is born to blush unseen,
   And waste its sweetness on the desert air.

(Gray, 'Country Churchyard')

Fŭll mă- | nў ă gém | ŏf púr- | ĕst ráy | sĕ-réne,

   Thĕ dárk | ŭn-fá- | thŏm'd cáves | ŏf ó- | cĕan béar:

Fŭll má- | nў ă flów'r | ĭs bórn | tŏ blúsh | ŭn-séen,

   Ănd wáste | ĭts swéet- | nĕss ón | thĕ dé- | sĕrt áir.

This passage is set in iambic pentameter. The first line has an anapaest in its second foot. The third line, too, has an anapaest in its second foot.

Behold her, single in the field,
Yon solitary Highland Lass!
Reaping and singing by herself;
Stop here, or gently pass! (Wordsworth, 'The Solitary Reaper')

Bĕ-hóld | hĕr, sín- | glĕ ín | thĕ fíeld,

Yŏn só- | lĭ-tá- | rў Hígh- | lănd Láss!

Réap-ĭng | ănd síng- | ĭng bý | hĕr-sélf;

Stóp hĕre, | ŏr gént- | lў páss!

The dominant metre of these lines is iambic tetrameter; however, the last line is trimetric. The first feet of the third line and the fourth line feature trochaic inversions.

No Nightingale did ever chaunt
More welcome notes to weary bands
Of travellers in some shady haunt,
Among Arabian sands:
A voice so thrilling ne'er was heard
In spring-time from the Cuckoo-bird,
Breaking the silence of the seas
Among the farthest Hebrides. (Wordsworth, 'The Solitary Reaper')

Nŏ Nígh- | tĭn-gále | dĭd év- | ĕr cháunt

Mŏre wél- | cŏme nótes | tŏ wéa- | rў bánds

Ŏf trá- | vĕl-lers ín | sŏme shá- | dў háunt,

Ă-móng | Ă-rá- | bĭan sánds:

Ă vóice | sŏ thríl- | lĭng né'er | wăs héard

Ĭn spríng- | tĭme fróm | thĕ Cúc- | kŏo-bírd,

Bréak-ĭng | thĕ sí- | lĕnce óf | thĕ séas

Ă-móng | thĕ fár- | thĕst Héb- | rĭ-dés.

The passage is composed in iambic tetrameter. The fourth line is trimetric. There is an anapaestic substitution in the second foot of the third line, and the first foot of the seventh line is a trochee. The rhyme scheme of the verse passage is *ababccdd*.

Earth has not anything to show more fair:
Dull would he be of soul who could pass by
A sight so touching in its majesty:
This City now doth, like a garment, wear
The beauty of the morning; silent, bare,
Ships, towers, domes, theatres, and temples lie
Open unto the fields, and to the sky;
All bright and glittering in the smokeless air.

(Wordsworth, 'Upon Westminster Bridge')

Éarth hăs | nŏt á- | nў-thĭng | tŏ shów | mŏre fáir:

Dúll wŏuld | hĕ bé | ŏf sóul | whŏ cóuld | páss bў

Ă síght | sŏ tóuch- | ĭng ín | ĭts má- | jĕs-tў:

Thĭs Cí- | tў nów | dŏth, líke | ă gár- | mĕnt, wéar

Thĕ béau- | tў óf | thĕ mórn- | ĭng; sí- | lĕnt, báre,

Shíps, tów- | ĕrs, dómes, | théa-trĕs, | ănd tém- | plĕs líe

Ó-pĕn | ún-tŏ | thĕ fíelds, | ănd tó | thĕ ský;

Ăll bríght | ănd glít- | tĕr-ĭng ín | thĕ smóke- | lĕss aír.

Wordsworth has thrown in several variations in his iambic pentameter lines. Trochees can be found in the first foot of the first line, the first foot of the second line, the third foot of the sixth line, and in the first two feet of the seventh line. The sixth line has a spondee in its first foot, while the third foot of the last line is anapaestic. The rhyme scheme is *abba abba*.

———————

The boast of heraldry, the pomp of pow'r,
    And all that beauty, all that wealth e'er gave,
Awaits alike th' inevitable hour:—
    The paths of glory lead but to the grave.
                              (Gray, 'Country Churchyard')

Thĕ bóast | ŏf hé- | rál-drў, | thĕ pómp | ŏf pów'r,

    Ănd áll | thăt beáu- | tў, áll | thăt wéalth | é'er gáve,

Ă-waíts | ă-líke | th' ĭn-év- | ĭt-á- | blĕ hóur:—

    Thĕ páths | ŏf gló- | rў léad | bŭt tó | thĕ gráve.

This stanza is in iambic pentameter, with an anapaestic variation in the third foot of the third line.

———————

Never did sun more beautifully steep
In his first splendour, valley, rock, or hill;
Ne'er saw I, never felt, a calm so deep!
The river glideth at his own sweet will:
Dear God! the very houses seem asleep;
And all that mighty heart is lying still!
                    (Wordsworth, 'Upon Westminster Bridge')

Né-vĕr | dĭd sún | mŏre beáu- | tĭ-fŭl- | lў stéep

Ĭn hís | fírst splén- | dŏur, vál- | lĕy, róck, | ŏr híll;

Nĕ'er săw | Ĭ, nĕ- | vĕr félt, | ă cálm | sŏ deép!

Thĕ rí- | vĕr glí- | dĕth át | hĭs ówn | sweét wíll:

Deár Gód! | thĕ vé- | rў hoús- | ĕs seém | ă-sleép;

Ănd áll | thăt mígh- | tў heárt | ĭs lý- | ĭng stíll!

The given lines are in iambic pentameter, with some variations in the rhythm. The first and third lines begin with a trochaic substitution. The first foot of the second line is pyrrhic. There are spondees in the second line (second foot), fourth line (fifth foot), and fifth line (first foot).

   Point out the rhyme scheme of the above lines.

_____

It is an ancient Mariner,
And he stoppeth one of three.
By thy long grey beard and glittering eye,
Now wherefore stop'st thou me?
                                   (Coleridge, 'Rime of the Ancient Mariner')

Ĭt ís | ăn án- | cĭent Má- | rĭ-nér,

Ănd hĕ stóp- | pĕth óne | ŏf threé.

Bў thў lóng | grĕy beárd | ănd glít- | tĕr-ĭng éye,

Nŏw whére- | fŏre stópp'st | thŏu mé?

The verse is in ballad metre—alternate lines of iambic tetrameter and iambic trimeter—with some variations. The second and third lines begin with anapaestic feet. The third line ends with an anapaest. The second and fourth lines rhyme with each other; the first and third lines do not rhyme with any line.

_____

Day after day, day after day,
We stuck, nor breath nor motion;
As idle as a painted ship
Upon a painted ocean.   (Coleridge, 'Rime of the Ancient Mariner')

Day áf- | tĕr dáy, | dáy áf- | tĕr dáy,

Wĕ stúck, | nŏr bréath | nŏr mó- | tiŏn;

Ăs í- | dlĕ ás | ă páin- | tĕd shíp

Ŭ-pón | ă páin- | tĕd ó- | cĕan.

Iambic tetrameter and iambic trimeter lines alternate in this stanza. The first line has two spondees: in the first and in the third feet. The second and fourth lines are hypermetrical.

NOTE

Look at the number of stressed syllables that Coleridge has put into the first line. These retard the rhythm, making it clunky, slow and laborious—which is exactly what the poet intended, because it matches the sense of the stanza (which talks about a frustrating lack of appreciable movement). This is an example of how skilled metrists manipulate rhythm to add layers of meaning to verse.

Haply some hoary-headed swain may say,
 Oft have we seen him at the peep of dawn
Brushing with hasty steps the dews away
 To meet the sun upon the upland lawn

        (Gray, 'Country Churchyard')

Háp-lў | sŏme hóa- | rў-héad- | ĕd swáin | măy sáy,

Óft hăve | wĕ séen | hĭm át | thĕ péep | ŏf dáwn

Brúsh-ĭng | wĭth hás- | tў stéps | thĕ déws | ă-wáy

Tŏ méet | thĕ sún | ŭ-pón | thĕ úp- | lănd láwn

The above verse passage is in iambic pentameter. The first, second and third lines begin with trochaic feet.
 What is such a stanza called?

Water, water, every where,
And all the boards did shrink;
Water, water, every where,
Nor any drop to drink.   (Coleridge, 'Rime of the Ancient Mariner')

Wa-ter, | wa-ter, | eve-ry | where,

And all | the boards | did shrink;

Wa-ter, | wa-ter, | eve-ry | where,

Nor a- | ny drop | to drink.

The first and third lines are trochaic tetrameter catalectic. The second and fourth lines are iambic trimeter.

The western wave was all aflame,
The day was well nigh done!
Almost upon the western wave
Rested the broad, bright Sun;
When that strange shape drove suddenly
Betwixt us and the Sun.   (Coleridge, 'Rime of the Ancient Mariner')

The west- | ern wave | was all | aflame,

The day | was well | nigh done!

Al-most | u-pon | the west- | ern wave

Res-ted | the broad, | bright Sun;

When that | strange shape | drove sud- | den-ly

Be-twixt | us and | the Sun.

The first, third and fifth lines are iambic tetrameter; the second, fourth and sixth lines are iambic trimeter. The first foot of the fourth line is a trochee. The second foot of the fifth line is a spondee.

Her lips were red, her looks were free,
Her locks were yellow as gold:
Her skin was as white as leprosy,
The Nightmare Life-in-Death was she,
Who thicks man's blood with cold.
                    (Coleridge, 'Rime of the Ancient Mariner')

Her lips| were red,| her looks| were free,

Her locks| were yel-| low as gold:

Her skin| was as white| as le-| pro-sy,

The Night-| mare Life-| in-Death| was she,

Who thicks| man's blood| with cold.

The first, third and fourth lines are iambic tetrameter; the second and fifth are iambic trimeter. The third foot of the second line and the second foot of the third line are anapaestic.

Alone, alone, all, all alone,
Alone on a wide, wide sea!
And never a saint took pity on
My soul in agony.   (Coleridge, 'Rime of the Ancient Mariner')

A-lone,| a-lone,| all, all| a-lone,

A-lone| on a wide,| wide sea!

And ne-| ver a saint| took pi-| ty on

My soul| in a-| go-ny.

Iambic tetrameter and iambic trimeter alternate in this stanza. The third feet of the first and second lines are spondees. The second feet of the second and third lines are anapaestic.

The moving Moon went up the sky,
And nowhere did abide;
Softly she was going up,
And a star or two beside
(Coleridge, 'Rime of the Ancient Mariner')

˘ ´ | ˘ ´ | ˘ ´ | ˘ ´
The mov- | ing Moon | went up | the sky,

˘ ´ | ˘ ´ | ˘ ´
And no | where did | a-bide;

´ ˘ | ´ ˘ | ´ ˘ | ´
Soft- | ly she | was go- | ing up,

˘ ˘ ´ | ˘ ´ | ˘ ´
And a star | or two | be-side

Coleridge alternates iambic tetrameter and trimeter in these lines. The third line is acephalous. The first foot of the last line is an anapaest.

He prayeth best, who loveth best
All things both great and small;
For the dear God who loveth us,
He made and loveth all. (Coleridge, 'Rime of the Ancient Mariner')

˘ ´ | ˘ ´ | ˘ ´ | ˘ ´
He pray- | eth best, | who lov- | eth best

˘ ´ | ˘ ´ | ˘ ´
All things | both great | and small;

˘ ˘ | ´ ´ | ˘ ´ | ˘ ´
For the | dear God | who lov- | eth us,

˘ ´ | ˘ ´ | ˘ ´
He made | and lov- | eth all.

The given passage is composed of alternating iambic tetrameter and iambic trimeter lines. The first foot of the third line is a pyrrhic, while the second foot is a spondee.

In Xanadu did Kubla Khan
A stately pleasure-dome decree:
Where Alph, the sacred river, ran
Through caverns measureless to man
    Down to a sunless sea. (Coleridge, 'Kubla Khan')

˘ ′ ˘ ′ ˘ ′ ˘ ′
In Xa- | na-du | did Kub- | la Khan

˘ ′ ˘ ′ ˘ ′ ˘ ′
A state- | ly plea- | sure-dome | de-cree:

˘ ′ ˘ ′ ˘ ′ ˘ ′
Where Alph, | the sac- | red ri- | ver, ran

˘ ′ ˘ ′ ˘ ′ ˘ ′
Through ca- | verns mea- | sure-less | to man

′ ˘ ˘ ′ ˘ ′
Down to | a sun- | less sea.

These lines of verse are set in iambic tetrameter. The last line of
the given passage, however, is iambic trimeter, and has a trochaic
substitution in its first foot.

———————

I bring fresh showers for the thirsting flowers,
   From the seas and the streams;
I bear light shade for the leaves when laid
   In their noonday dreams.
From my wings are shaken the dews that waken
   The sweet buds every one,
When rocked to rest on their mother's breast,
   As she dances about the sun.   (Shelley, 'The Cloud')

˘ ′ ˘ ′ ˘ ˘ ′ ˘ ′ ˘
I bring | fresh show(e)rs | for the thirst- | ing flo | wers,

˘ ˘ ′ ˘ ˘ ′
   From the seas | and the streams;

˘ ′ ˘ ′ ˘ ˘ ′ ˘ ′
I bear | light shade | for the leaves | when laid

˘ ˘ ′ ˘ ′
   In their noon- | day dreams.

˘ ˘ ′ ˘ ′ ˘ ˘ ′ ˘ ′ ˘
From my wings | are shak- | en the dews | that wa- | ken

˘ ′ ˘ ˘ ′ ˘ ′
   The sweet | buds eve- | ry one,

˘ ′ ˘ ′ ˘ ˘ ′ ˘ ′
When rocked | to rest | on their mo- | ther's breast,

˘ ˘ ′ ˘ ˘ ′ ˘ ′
   As she dan- | ces a-bout | the sun.

These lines are in mixed iambic and anapaestic metre, and may be
scanned as follows—

Line 1: iambic tetrameter hypermetrical, with an elision in the second foot, and the third foot anapaestic

Line 2: anapaestic dimeter

Line 3: iambic tetrameter, with the third foot anapaestic

Line 4: anapaestic dimeter, with the second foot iambic

Line 5: iambic tetrameter hypermetrical, with the first and the third feet anapaestic

Line 6: iambic trimeter

Line 7: iambic tetrameter, with the third foot anapaestic

Line 8: anapaestic trimeter, with the third foot iambic

In this poem, Shelley mixes two rising metres (iamb and anapaest), throws in plenty of substitutions, and even varies line lengths—which is very apt given the free-spirited protean nature of the narrator persona (a cloud) and for poem's joyous tone. The poem is a delightful experiment in controlled disorder, and its focus is on music rather than on metre.

NOTE

An **elision** is the muting or omission of an unstressed vowel or consonant sound in a word. Elisions are common in spoken language, particularly in informal speech. For example, 'family' (fa-*mi*-ly) often gets shortened to '*fam*-ly'; and 'vegetable' (ve-*ji*-tuh-buhl) becomes '*vej*-tuh-buhl'.

Poets often use elision to make words fit into the metrical scheme of their verse. In writing, the letter representing the elided sound is substituted by an apostrophe; for example, heaven → heav'n; never → ne'er; and so on.

———

The Bridegroom's doors are opened wide,
And I am next of kin;
The guests are met, the feast is set:
May'st hear the merry din.

> (Coleridge, 'Rime of the Ancient Mariner')

The Bride- |groom's doors |are o- |pened wide,

And I |am next |of kin;

The guests |are met, |the feast |is set:

May'st hear |the mer- |ry din.

The first and third lines are in iambic tetrameter; the second and fourth, in iambic trimeter. The second foot of the first line is spondaic.

———————

The sanguine sunrise, with his meteor eyes,
  And his burning plumes outspread,
Leaps on the back of my sailing rack,
  When the morning star shines dead,
As on the jag of a mountain crag,
  Which an earthquake rocks and swings,
An eagle alit one moment may sit
  In the light of its golden wings.   (Shelley, 'The Cloud')

The san- |guine sun-rise, |with his me- |teor eyes,

  And his bur- |ning plumes |out-spread,

Leaps on |the back |of my sail- |ing rack,

  When the morn- |ing star |shines dead,

As on |the jag |of a moun- |tain crag,

  Which an earth- |quake rocks |and swings,

An ea- |gle a-lit |one mo- |ment may sit

  In the light |of its gold- |en wings.

The dominant metre is iambic, with alternate tetrameter and trimeter lines. The variations are as follows—

Line 1: amphibrachic second foot; anapaestic third foot
Line 2: anapaestic first foot
Line 3: trochaic first foot; anapaestic third foot
Line 4: anapaestic first foot
Line 5: trochaic first foot; anapaestic third foot
Line 6: anapaestic first foot
Line 7: anapaestic second foot; anapaestic fourth foot
Line 8: anapaestic first foot; anapaestic second foot

I bind the sun's throne with a burning zone,
  And the moon's with a girdle of pearl;
The volcanoes are dim, and the stars reel and swim,
  When the whirlwinds my banner unfurl. (Shelley, 'The Cloud')

I bind | the sun's throne | with a burn- | ing zone,

  And the moon's | with a gir- | dle of pearl;

The vol-ca- | noes are dim, | and the stars | reel and swim,

  When the whirl- | winds my ban- | ner un-furl.

This passage has alternate lines of anapaestic tetrameter and anapaestic trimeter. The first and the fourth feet of the first line are iambic.

Note that the third line may also be scanned as—

  The vol-ca- | noes are dim, | and the | stars reel | and swim

---

I am the daughter of earth and water,
  And the nursling of the sky;
I pass through the pores of the ocean and shores;
  I change, but I cannot die. (Shelley, 'The Cloud')

I am | the daugh- | ter of earth | and wa- | ter,

  And the nurs- | ling of | the sky;

I pass | through the pores | of the o- | cean and shores;

  I change, | but I can- | not die.

The dominant metre is iambic, with alternate tetrameter and trimeter lines. The variations are as follows—

Line 1: trochaic first foot; anapaestic third foot; hypermetrical
        line
Line 2: anapaestic first foot
Line 3: anapaestic second, third and fourth feet
Line 4: anapaestic second foot

I silently laugh at my own cenotaph,
　And out of the caverns of rain,
Like a child from the womb, like a ghost from the tomb,
　I arise and unbuild it again.　(Shelley, 'The Cloud')

```
˘  ´     ˘    ˘  ´      ˘    ˘ ´     ˘  ˘  ´
I si- | lent-ly laugh | at my own | ce-no-taph,

     ˘    ´   ˘   ˘  ´   ˘    ˘   ´
　And out | of the ca- | verns of rain,

˘   ˘   ´    ˘    ˘   ´   ˘   ˘   ´    ˘    ˘ ´
Like a child | from the womb, | like a ghost | from the tomb,

     ˘˘  ´    ˘   ˘   ´   ˘˘  ´
　I a-rise | and un-build | it a-gain.
```

The dominant metre of these verse lines is anapaestic, with alternating tetrameter and trimeter lines. The first feet of the first two lines are iambic.

When the lamp is shattered
The light in the dust lies dead—
When the cloud is scattered
The rainbow's glory is shed.　(Shelley, 'When the Lamp is Shattered')

```
´    ˘   ´  ˘    ´  ˘
When the | lamp is | shat-tered

˘   ´    ˘  ˘   ´   ˘   ´
The light | in the dust | lies dead—

´    ˘   ´  ˘   ´  ˘
When the | cloud is | scat-tered

˘   ´    ˘   ´   ˘˘   ´
The rain- | bow's glo- | ry is shed.
```

These lines are in mixed trochaic and iambic trimeter, with the first and third lines in trochaic metre, and the other two in iambic metre. The second foot of the second line is an anapaest. The third foot of the fourth line is also an anapaest.

My heart aches, and a drowsy numbness pains
　My sense, as though of hemlock I had drunk,
Or emptied some dull opiate to the drains
　One minute past, and Lethe-wards had sunk.
　　　　　　　　　(Keats, 'Ode to a Nightingale')

My heart| aches, and| a drow-| sy numb-| ness pains

   My sense,| as though| of hem-| lock I| had drunk,

Or emp-| tied some| dull o-| pi-ate| to the drains

   One min-| ute past,| and Le-| the-wards| had sunk.

This passage is written in iambic pentameter. There is a trochaic substitution in the second foot of the first line. The final foot of the third line is anapaestic.

———

Heard melodies are sweet, but those unheard
   Are sweeter; therefore, ye soft pipes, play on;
Not to the sensual ear, but, more endear'd,
   Pipe to the spirit ditties of no tone.

                   (Keats, 'Ode on a Grecian Urn')

Heard me-| lo-dies| are sweet,| but those| un-heard

   Are sweet-| er; there-| fore, ye| soft pipes,| play on;

Not to| the sen-| sual ear,| but, more| en-dear'd,

   Pipe to| the spi-| rit dit-| ties of| no tone.

These lines have been composed in iambic pentameter. The first line begins with a spondee, followed by a pyrrhic. The fourth foot of the second line is a spondee. The third and fourth lines begin with a trochaic inversion.

———

Roll on, thou deep and dark blue Ocean, roll!
Ten thousand fleets sweep over thee in vain;
Man marks the earth with ruin; his control
Stops with the shore; upon the watery plain

               (Byron, *Childe Harold's Pilgrimage*)

Roll on,| thou deep| and dark| blue O-| cean, roll!

Ten thou-| sand fleets| sweep o-| ver thee| in vain;

Man marks| the earth| with ru-| in; his| con-trol

Stops with| the shore;| u-pon| the wa-| te-ry plain

The given lines are in iambic pentameter, with a few variations. The first foot of the first line is trochaic. The third foot of the second line is a spondee. The final line begins with a trochee and ends with an anapaest.

———————

Sunset and evening star,
And one clear call for me!
And may there be no moaning of the bar,
When I put out to sea   (Tennyson, 'Crossing the Bar')

Sun-set| and eve-| ning star,

And one| clear call| for me!

And may| there be| no moan-| ing of| the bar,

When I| put out| to sea

The dominant metrical pattern is iambic trimeter; however, the third line is in iambic pentameter. The first foot of the first line is trochaic. The second foot of the second line is spondaic.

———————

The sea is calm to-night.
The tide is full, the moon lies fair
Upon the straits; on the French coast the light
Gleams and is gone; the cliffs of England stand,
Glimmering and vast, out in the tranquil bay.

(Arnold, 'Dover Beach')

The sea| is calm| to-night.

The tide| is full,| the moon| lies fair

U-pon| the straits;| on the| French coast| the light

Gleams and | is gone; | the cliffs | of Eng- | land stand,

Glimm(e)-ring | and vast, | out in | the tran- | quil bay.

The dominant metre of these lines is iambic.

Line 1: iambic trimeter
Line 2: iambic tetrameter; the last foot is a spondee
Line 3: iambic pentameter; the third and fourth feet are pyrrhic and spondaic respectively
Line 4: iambic pentameter; the first foot is trochaic
Line 5: iambic pentameter; the first foot is trochaic, with the elision of an unstressed syllable

NOTE

Since Arnold has not indicated that the word 'glimmering' (in the last line) should be elided to 'glimm'ring', the final line may also be scanned as follows:

Glim-me-ring | and vast, | out in | the tran- | quil bay

...that is, with a dactyl in the first foot. Dactylic feet are rare in iambic and anapaestic metres, and may occur only in the first feet of rising metres.

When you are old and grey and full of sleep,
And nodding by the fire, take down this book,
And slowly read, and dream of the soft look
Your eyes had once, and of their shadows deep
(Yeats, 'When You Are Old')

When you | are old | and grey | and full | of sleep,

And nod- | ding by | the fire, | take down | this book,

And slow- | ly read, | and dream | of the | soft look

Your eyes | had once, | and of | their sha- | dows deep

This passage is in iambic pentameter with a few variations. In the third line, the fourth foot is pyrrhic, while the last foot is spondaic. In the third line, the third foot is pyrrhic.

Exercises

Scan the following verse passages: name the metre and mention the variations.

From 'One Day I Wrote Her Name', Edmund Spenser

1. One day I wrote her name upon the strand,
   But came the waves and washéd it away:
   Again I wrote it with a second hand,
   But came the tide, and made my pains his prey.

From 'Sonnet 18', William Shakespeare

2. Shall I compare thee to a summer's day?
   Thou art more lovely and more temperate:
   Rough winds do shake the darling buds of May,
   And summer's lease hath all too short a date.

From 'Lycidas', John Milton

3. Yet once more, O ye laurels, and once more
   Ye myrtles brown, with ivy never sere,
   I come to pluck your berries harsh and crude,
   And with forced fingers rude
   Shatter your leaves before the mellowing year.

4. Bitter constraint and sad occasion dear
   Compels me to disturb your season due;
   For Lycidas is dead, dead ere his prime,
   Young Lycidas, and hath not left his peer.

5. The willows and the hazel copses green
   Shall now no more be seen
   Fanning their joyous leaves to thy soft lays.
   As killing as the canker to the rose,

Or taint-worm to the weanling herds that graze,
Or frost to flowers, that their gay wardrobe wear,
When first the white-thorn blows:
Such, Lycidas, thy loss to shepherd's ear.

6. What could the Muse herself that Orpheus bore,
The Muse herself, for her inchanting son,
Whom universal nature did lament,
When, by the rout that made the hideous roar
His gory visage down the stream was sent,
Down the swift Hebrus to the Lesbian shore?

From 'A Valediction: Forbidding Mourning', John Donne

7. So let us melt, and make no noise,
　　No tear-floods, nor sigh-tempests move;
'Twere profanation of our joys
　　To tell the laity our love.

8. But we, by a love so much refined,
　　That ourselves know not what it is,
Inter-assuréd of the mind,
　　Careless, eyes, lips and hands to miss.

9. If they be two, they are two so
　　As stiff twin compasses are two;
Thy soul, the fixt foot, makes no show
　　To move, but doth, if th' other do.

From 'Horatian Ode upon Cromwell's Return from Ireland',
Andrew Marvell

10. So restless Cromwell could not cease
In the inglorious arts of peace,
　　　But through adventerous war
　　　Urgéd his active star.

11. 'Tis madness to resist or blame
The force of angry Heaven's flame;
　　　And if we would speak true,
　　　Much to the man is due,
Who, from his private gardens, where
He lived reservéd and austere

12. Nor call'd the gods, with vulgar spite,
    To vindicate his helpless right;
        But bow'd his comely head
        Down as upon a bed.
    —This was that memorable hour
    Which first assured the forcéd power.

From 'The Tyger', William Blake

13. Tyger Tyger, burning bright,
    In the forests of the night,
    What immortal hand or eye
    Could frame thy fearful symmetry?

14. In what distant deeps or skies
    Burnt the fire of thine eyes?
    On what wings dare he aspire?
    What the hand, dare seize the fire?

15. What the hammer? what the chain,
    In what furnace was thy brain?
    What the anvil? what dread grasp
    Dare its deadly terrors clasp!

16. When the stars threw down their spears
    And water'd heaven with their tears,
    Did He smile his work to see?
    Did He who made the Lamb make thee?

From 'To the Daisy', William Wordsworth

17. Methinks that there abides in thee
    Some concord with humanity,
    Given to no other flower I see
        The forest thorough!

18. Is it that Man is soon deprest?
    A thoughtless Thing! who, once unblest,
    Does little on his memory rest,
        Or on his reason,
    And Thou would'st teach him how to find
    A shelter under every wind,
    A hope for times that are unkind
        And every season?

From 'The World Is Too Much With Us', William Wordsworth

19. The World is too much with us; late and soon,
     Getting and spending, we lay waste our powers:
     Little we see in Nature that is ours;
     We have given our hearts away, a sordid boon!

20. It moves us not.—Great God! I'd rather be
     A pagan suckled in a creed outworn,—
     So might I, standing on this pleasant lea,
     Have glimpses that would make me less forlorn

From 'Christabel', Samuel Taylor Coleridge

21. 'Tis the middle of night by the castle clock,
     And the owls have awakened the crowing cock;
     Tu—whit! Tu—whoo!
     And hark, again! the crowing cock,
     How drowsily it crew!

22. The moon is behind, and at the full;
     And yet she looks both small and dull.
     The night is chill, the cloud is gray:
     'Tis a month before the month of May,
     And the Spring comes slowly up this way.

23. She stole along, she nothing spoke,
     The sighs she heaved were soft and low,
     And naught was green upon the oak
     But moss and rarest misletoe:
     She kneels beneath the huge oak-tree,
     And in silence prayeth she.

24. There she sees a damsel bright,
     Drest in a silken robe of white,
     That shadowy in the moonlight shone:
     The neck that made that white robe wan,
     Her stately neck, and arms were bare;
     Her blue-veined feet unsandlled were,
     And wildly glittered here and there
     The gems entangled in her hair.

From 'To a Skylark', Percy Bysshe Shelley

25.   The pale purple even
          Melts around thy flight;
      Like a star of heaven,
          In the broad daylight
Thou art unseen, but yet I hear thy shrill delight

26.   Like a poet hidden
          In the light of thought,
      Singing hymns unbidden,
          Till the world is wrought
To sympathy with hopes and fears it heeded not

27.   We look before and after,
          And pine for what is not:
      Our sincerest laughter
          With some pain is fraught;
Our sweetest songs are those that tell of saddest thought.

28.   Teach me half the gladness
          That thy brain must know;
      Such harmonious madness
          From my lips would flow
The world should listen then, as I am listening now.

From 'Mutability', Percy Bysshe Shelley

29. We are as clouds that veil the midnight moon;
    How restlessly they speed and gleam and quiver,
    Streaking the darkness radiantly! yet soon
    Night closes round, and they are lost for ever

30. We rest—a dream has power to poison sleep;
    We rise—one wandering thought pollutes the day;
    We feel, conceive or reason, laugh or weep,
    Embrace fond woe, or cast our cares away

From 'The Indian Serenade', Percy Bysshe Shelley

31. I arise from dreams of thee
    In the first sweet sleep of night,

When the winds are breathing low,
And the stars are shining bright.

32. Oh lift me from the grass!
     I die! I faint! I fail!
     Let thy love in kisses rain
     On my lips and eyelids pale.

33. My cheek is cold and white, alas!
     My heart beats loud and fast:
     O press it to thine own again,
     Where it will break at last!

From *Endymion*, John Keats

34. A thing of beauty is a joy for ever:
     Its loveliness increases; it will never
     Pass into nothingness; but still will keep
     A bower quiet for us, and a sleep
     Full of sweet dreams, and health, and quiet breathing.

35. We have imagined for the mighty dead;
     All lovely tales that we have heard or read:
     An endless fountain of immortal drink,
     Pouring unto us from the heaven's brink.

From 'Ulysses', Alfred, Lord Tennyson

36. Much have I seen and known; cities of men
     And manners, climates, councils, governments,
     Myself not least, but honour'd of them all;
     And drunk delight of battle with my peers,
     Far on the ringing plains of windy Troy.

37. The long day wanes: the slow moon climbs: the deep
     Moans round with many voices. Come, my friends,
     'Tis not too late to seek a newer world.
     Push off, and sitting well in order smite
     The sounding furrows; for my purpose holds
     To sail beyond the sunset, and the baths
     Of all the western stars, until I die.

From *In Memoriam*, Alfred Tennyson

38. I envy not the beast that takes
          His license in the field of time,
          Unfetter'd by the sense of crime,
     To whom a conscience never wakes

39. I hold it true, whate'er befall;
          I feel it, when I sorrow most;
          'Tis better to have loved and lost
     Than never to have loved at all.

From 'The Last Ride Together', Robert Browning

40. I said—Then, dearest, since 'tis so,
     Since now at length my fate I know,
     Since nothing all my love avails,
     Since all, my life seem'd meant for, fails,
     Since this was written and needs must be—
     My whole heart rises up to bless
     Your name in pride and thankfulness!

41. Hush! if you saw some western cloud
     All billowy-bosom'd, over-bow'd
     By many benedictions—sun's
     And moon's, and evening-star's at once

42. What need to strive with a life awry?
     Had I said that, had I done this,
     So might I gain, so might I miss.
     Might she have loved me? just as well
     She might have hated, who can tell!

43. Fail I alone, in words and deeds?
     Why, all men strive and who succeeds?
     We rode; it seem'd my spirit flew,
     Saw other regions, cities new
     As the world rush'd by on either side.

From 'The Scholar-Gipsy', Matthew Arnold

44. Here, where the reaper was at work of late—
     In this high field's dark corner, where he leaves

His coat, his basket, and his earthen cruse,
And in the sun all morning binds the sheaves,
Then here, at noon, comes back his stores to use—
Here will I sit and wait

45. And near me on the grass lies Glanvil's book—
Come, let me read the oft-read tale again!
The story of the Oxford scholar poor,
Of pregnant parts and quick inventive brain,
Who, tired of knocking at preferment's door,
One summer-morn forsook
His friends, and went to learn the gipsy-lore

46. At some lone homestead in the Cumner hills,
Where at her open door the housewife darns,
Thou hast been seen, or hanging on a gate
To watch the threshers in the mossy barns.

47. Thou hast not lived, why should'st thou perish, so?
Thou hadst *one* aim, *one* business, *one* desire;
Else wert thou long since number'd with the dead!
Else hadst thou spent, like other men, thy fire!
The generations of thy peers are fled,
And we ourselves shall go;
But thou possessest an immortal lot

From 'The Blessed Damozel', Dante Gabriel Rossetti

48. Her eyes were deeper than the depth
Of waters still'd at even;
She had three lilies in her hand,
And the stars in her hair were seven.

49. The sun was gone now; the curl'd moon
Was like a little feather
Fluttering far down the gulf; and now
She spoke through the still weather.

50. She gazed and listen'd and then said,
Less sad of speech than mild,—
'All this is when he comes.' She ceas'd.
The light thrill'd towards her, fill'd

With angels in strong level flight.
Her eyes pray'd, and she smil'd

From 'The Darkling Thrush', Thomas Hardy

51. The land's sharp features seem'd to be
    The Century's corpse outleant,
His crypt the cloudy canopy,
    The wind his death-lament.

52. The ancient pulse of germ and birth
    Was shrunken hard and dry,
And every spirit upon earth
    Seem'd fervourless as I.

53. An aged thrush, frail, gaunt, and small,
    In blast-beruffled plume,
Had chosen thus to fling his soul
    Upon the growing gloom.

From 'Fern Hill', Dylan Thomas

54. And as I was green and carefree, famous among the barns
About the happy yard and singing as the farm was home,
    In the sun that is young once only,
        Time let me play and be
    Golden in the mercy of his means,
And green and golden I was huntsman and herdsman, the calves
Sang to my horn, the foxes on the hills barked clear and cold,
    And the sabbath rang slowly
    In the pebbles of the holy streams.

From 'Stopping by Woods on a Snowy Evening', Robert Frost

55. Whose woods these are I think I know.
His house is in the village though;
He will not see me stopping here
To watch his woods fill up with snow.

56. My little horse must think it queer
     To stop without a farmhouse near
     Between the woods and frozen lake
     The darkest evening of the year.

57. The woods are lovely, dark and deep,
     But I have promises to keep,
     And miles to go before I sleep,
     And miles to go before I sleep.

From 'The Brain is Wider than the Sky', Emily Dickinson

58. The brain is wider than the sky,
     For, put them side by side,
     The one the other will include
     With ease, and you beside.

From 'Hope is the Thing with Feathers', Emily Dickinson

59. 'Hope' is the thing with feathers
     That perches in the soul
     And sings the tune without the words
     And never stops—at all.

From 'Anthem for Doomed Youth', Wilfred Owen

60. What candles may be held to speed them all?
     Not in the hands of boys but in their eyes
     Shall shine the holy glimmers of goodbyes.
     The pallor of girls' brows shall be their pall;
     Their flowers the tenderness of patient minds,
     And each slow dusk a drawing-down of blinds.

References

Alexander, Gavin. 'Prosopopoeia: The Speaking Figure'. *Renaissance Figures of Speech*. Ed. Sylvia Adamson, et al. Cambridge: Cambridge UP, 2007.

Aristotle. *On Rhetoric: A Theory of Civic Discourse*. Ed. and trans. George A. Kennedy. New York: Oxford UP, 1991.

Aristotle. *Rhetoric*. Trans. W. Rhys Roberts. Online. *The Internet Classics Archive*. http://classics.mit.edu/Aristotle/rhetoric.3.iii. html.

Bialostosky, Don H. and Lawrence D. Needham. *Rhetorical Traditions and British Romantic Literature*. Bloomington: Indiana UP, 1995.

Bloom, Harold. *The Anxiety of Influence: A Theory of Poetry*. London and New York: Oxford UP, 1975.

Brooks, Cleanth. *The Well Wrought Urn*. New York: Harcourt Brace, 1947.

Burke, Kenneth. *Language as Symbolic Action: Essays on Life, Literature, and Method*. Berkeley: U of California P, 1966.

——. *A Rhetoric of Motive*. Berkeley: U of California P, 1969.

Butler, H.E. Ed. *The Institutio Oratoria of Quintilian* (Vols. 1–4). 1921. Cambridge: Harvard UP, 1977.

Claridge, Claudia. *Hyperbole in English: A Corpus-based Study of Exaggeration*. Cambridge: Cambridge UP, 2011.

Comas, James. 'Rhetoric'. *Encyclopedia of Postmodernism*. Ed. Victor E. Taylor and Charles E. Winquist. London and New York: Routledge, 2001.

Conley, Thomas M. *Rhetoric in the European Tradition*. 1990. Chicago and London: U of Chicago P, 1994.

Culler, Jonathan. 'Apostrophe'. *The Pursuit of Signs: Semiotics, Literature, Deconstruction*. 1981. London and New York: Routledge, 2005.

De Man, Paul. *Resistance to Theory*. 1986. Minneapolis and London: U of Minnesota P, 2002.

Dillard, James P. and Michael Pfau. Ed. *The Persuasion Handbook: Developments in Theory and Practice*. Thousand Oaks, CA: Sage, 2002.

Fish, Stanley. 'Rhetoric'. *Doing What Comes Naturally: Change, Rhetoric and the Practice of Theory in Literary and Legal Studies*. 1989. Oxford: Clarendon, 2011.

Fraser, Bruce. 'An Account of Innuendo'. *Perspectives on Semantics, Pragmatics, and Discourse: A Festschrift for Ferenc Kiefer*. Ed. István Kenesei, et al. Amsterdam and Philadelphia: John Benjamins Publishing Company, 2001.

Goffman, Erving. *Interaction Ritual: Essays in Face-to-Face Behaviour*. 1967. London and New Brunswick: Aldine Transaction, 2005.

Golden, James and P.J. Corbett. Ed. *The Rhetoric of Blair, Campbell, and Whately*. 1968. Carbondale and Edwardsville: Southern Illinois UP, 1990.

Habinek, Thomas. *Ancient Rhetoric and Oratory*. Malden, MA: Blackwell, 2005.

Hunt, E.L. 'On the Sophists'. *The Province of Rhetoric*. Ed. J. Schwartz and J.A. Rycenga. New York: Ronald Press, 1965.

Hunter, William. Ed. *Milton's English Poetry: Being Entries from A Milton Encyclopaedia*. London and Toronto: Bucknell University Press, 1986.

Jarvie, Gordon. *Bloomsbury Grammar Guide: Grammar Made Easy*. 1993. London: A&C Black, 2009. 2nd ed.

Johnson, Samuel. 'Preface to Shakespeare'. *Prefaces and Prologues*. Vol. XXXIX. The Harvard Classics. New York: P.F. Collier & Son, 1909–14.

Kneale, J. Douglas. *Romantic Aversions: Aftermaths of Classicism in Wordsworth and Coleridge*. McGill-Queen's University Press, 1999. Online. *JSTOR*, www.jstor.org/stable/j.ctt812nd.

Lacan, Jacques. 'The Insistence of the Letter in the Unconscious'. Trans. Jan Miel. *Yale French Studies*, Vol 36/37, 1966: 112–147.

Longinus. *On the Sublime*. Trans. H.L. Havell. London: Macmillan and Co Ltd, 1890. Online. http://www.gutenberg.org/files/17957/17957-h/17957-h.htm.

Maguire, Laurie. *Othello: Language and Writing*. London and New York: Bloomsbury, 2014.

McFarland, Thomas. *Originality and Imagination*. Baltimore: Johns Hopkins UP, 1985.

Mikics, David. *A New Handbook of Literary Terms*. New Haven and London: Yale UP, 2007.

Miller, Hillis. 'Nietzsche in Basel: Writing Reading'. *Journal of Advanced Composition* 13:2 (Fall 1993): 311–28.

Nesfield, John C. *Manual of English Grammar and Composition*. London: Macmillan & Co Ltd, 1898.

Partridge, A.C. *The Language of Renaissance Poetry*. London: Andre Deutsch, 1971.

Peet, Malcolm and David Robinson. *Leading Questions*. Cheltenham: Thomas Nelson and Sons Ltd, 1992.

Quintilian. *On the Early Education of the Citizen-orator: Institutio Oratoria*. Trans. J.S. Watson. Ed. J.J. Murphy. Indianapolis: Bobbs-Merril, 1965.

Richards, Jennifer. *Rhetoric*. The New Critical Idiom Series. London and New York: Routledge, 2008.

Skinner, Quentin. *Reason and Rhetoric in the Philosophy of Hobbes*. Cambridge: Cambridge UP, 1996.